The Gro
Bruges

Irene Smets

THE GROENINGE MUSEUM, BRUGES
A Selection of the Finest Works

Ludion

PREFACE

The Groeninge Museum is undoubtedly one of the loveliest galleries in Europe. A new illustrated visitor's guide is, therefore, always more than welcome.
This publication has been produced by Ludion Press, which has collaborated with the Municipal Museums of Bruges on a number of earlier occasions, producing catalogues and other prestigious publications on Bruges' artistic heritage.

This museum, with its survey of six centuries of painting from Jan van Eyck to Marcel Broodthaers, abounds in material for an illustrated art book. This new, fresh and attractive Groeninge guide not only offers beautiful illustrations for museum-goers to enjoy after their visit, but also a highly readable and informative account of the works. The author, Irene Smets, discusses a large number of paintings and several sculptures perceptively and fluently. In so doing, she has made an up-to-date contribution to the historical study of Flemish art in a museum that is among the very best in Europe.

Dr V. Vermeersch
Chief Curator

p. 1 Pieter Pourbus, *Portrait of Jan van Eyewerve*,
detail (see p. 56)
p. 2 Hans Memling, *Triptych of Willem Moreel*,
detail (see p. 24)

Frits Van den Berghe, *Village Sweethearts*,
detail (see p. 108)

Few visitors to Bruges miss the opportunity to see the Groeninge Museum. This attractive museum in the heart of the historic city offers a survey of six centuries of art in the Southern Netherlands (Belgium), from Jan van Eyck to Marcel Broodthaers. The collection reflects the astonishing artistic creativity that has manifested itself in this small corner of Europe for century after century.

The collection's centre of gravity is undoubtedly the Old Masters department. This consists of the 15th-century Flemish 'Primitives' and the 16th-century 'Mannerists', who renewed the Flemish pictorial tradition under the influence of the Italian Renaissance. The fact that this unique ensemble is located in the city where a number of these masters lived and worked five centuries ago makes a visit to the Groeninge Museum an even more intense experience.

Bruges' response to Baroque and Classical art is followed by the many artistic movements of the 19th century.

Belgian art from 1900 to the present is another important strand within the collection. The nucleus is formed by an exceptional corpus of Flemish Expressionist paintings. Belgian Modernism is also represented through first-rate works by several leading artists. Finally, the museum boasts a unique and complete collection of Marcel Broodthaers' printed editions.

BRIEF HISTORY OF THE COLLECTION

1717	Foundation of an Academy of Fine Arts in Bruges: the 'Vrije ende exempte Confrerie van teecken- ende schilderconst'
18th century	The Academy gradually builds up a collection of work by contemporary Bruges painters
19th century	Several collections from public and religious buildings in Bruges are brought together at the Academy; there are also several donations and bequests
1875	Charles van Lede donation (45 paintings)
1892	The City Council takes over the collection from the Academy
1903	Foundation of the 'Friends of the Museums' association with the goal of expanding the collection
1904 and after	Donations from Mrs Charles van der Beeck-Bouvy (1904), Minister of State Auguste Beernaert (1913) and Baron Edouard Houtart (1926)
1929–30	Construction of the Groeninge Museum (architect Joseph Viérin) on the site of the former Eekhout Abbey, close to the Groeninge district. The municipal painting collection, with its world-famous early Netherlandish paintings, finally gets a proper home
1954	Aquilin Janssens de Bisthoven becomes the first full-time, academically trained curator
1955	Transfer of the Société Archéologique's collection to the city, which divides it between the Groeninge Museum (fine art) and the Gruuthuse Museum (decorative arts)
1982–83	New wing built to create additional space for the significantly growing group of 15th- and early 16th-century works
1986	Purchase of sixteen outstanding Flemish Expressionist works from the Tony Herbert collection
1994–95	Further expansion to house the modern art collection. The museum is linked to the adjacent neo-Gothic building designed in 1875 by the architect Jean-Baptiste Bethune for the Confraternity of St Francis Xavier (the 'Xavier Wing')

The Virgin and Child with Canon Joris van der Paele 1436
Jan van Eyck c. 1390–1441
Panel, 122.1 x 157.8 cm

'Master Joris van der Paele, canon of this church, had this painting made by Johannes van Eyck, painter; and he founded two chantries, to be tended by the canons, 1434; the painting was, however, completed in 1436.' So reads a Latin inscription on the frame. In other words, the canon donated a substantial sum of money to the authorities of St Donatian's Church in Bruges to dedicate an annual mass to his memory in perpetuity. The painting will have hung alongside or above the altar at which one of the foundations or chantries was located.

Joris van der Paele had worked as *scriptor* in the papal chancery in Rome, following which he managed to acquire a number of lucrative posts in the Church. He moved to Bruges, which was probably his native city, around 1425. Aged about 55, he was a wealthy, retired canon. Van der Paele died in 1443.

It is not easy to sum up this marvellous painting in a few sentences. Take your time, and use your eyes and empathy, and you will discover a great deal for yourself.

The donor of the panel is painted with astonishing realism. He does not look in the best of health and a doctor could diagnose his condition from this detailed portrait. Dressed in a white surplice, prayerbook in hand, he looks like he is taking part in a church service. Where the altar would normally be, however, we see the Virgin Mary enthroned with her Child. Two saints are also present – the former Bishop Donatian, patron saint of the church for which the panel was painted, and George,

the canon's patron saint. Donatian holds his staff and a cartwheel with burning candles – attributes that refer to his life story. St George presents the canon to Mary and Jesus. As he removes his helmet, he looks reassuringly at the Child. His mouth is half open, as if he is greeting Jesus. On the decorative breastplate of his armour, we make out the Greek word *Adonai* (Lord!). Jesus holds an Indian parakeet, a bird that could, it was believed, say 'Ave' (Hail). Mary and her Child thus appear to be welcoming the canon and his patron saint.

There is a great deal more symbolism in the painting. Donatian wears a blue cope, the Virgin a red cloak, the canon a white alb and George a suit of golden armour. Together, these are the heraldic colours of Bruges.

The robes and other fabrics are beautifully rendered. The armour gleams and even reflects objects outside the painting's field of view: in the elbow-protector, for instance, we can make out a window and the figures of several onlookers, while the shield on George's back clearly reflects a small group of people, with what is probably Jan van Eyck himself in the foreground.

The Latin texts on the frame of the painting relate to Mary and the two saints. The top of the frame contains a text from the *Wisdom of Solomon*: 'She is more beautiful than the sun, and exceeds every constellation of the stars. Compared with the light she is found to be superior, for she is a reflection of eternal light, a spotless mirror of the working of God.' Mary's glorious

Jan van Eyck achieves a perfect synthesis between earthly reality, which he observes down to the tiniest detail, and a mystical cosmos that reveals itself to humanity through physical things. He created this divine yet tangible universe using his refined oil-painting technique, in which the combination of the white ground with the transparency of colours applied in several thin glazes produced an unparalleled brightness and clarity.

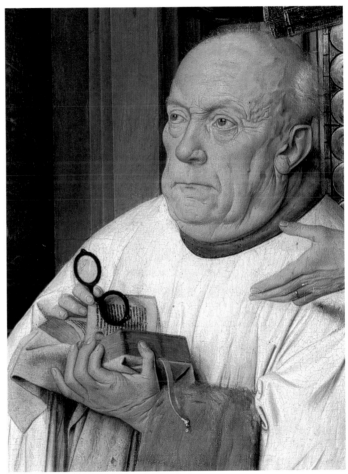

light fills the space and illuminates the figures, who stand like giants in the architectural setting.

To Van Eyck and his contemporaries, the visible world was a reflection of the divine – a belief to which he was able to give shape with exceptional artistic force. The mystical vision seems to have become reality. Inhabitants of heaven have come down to us. Like the canon and the little figures reflected in the shield, it is our privilege to gaze diffidently upon them.

Jan van Eyck was born around 1390, probably in Maaseik (then in the Prince-Bishopric of Liège, now in Belgium). He was appointed court painter to the Count of Holland in The Hague in 1422. Following the count's death in 1425, he came to Bruges, where he became court painter and chamberlain to Philip the Good, the powerful and art-loving Duke of Burgundy. His job was to 'make paintings such as will please the duke'. We only know of one work that Jan painted on behalf of the duke – a 1429 portrait, now lost, of Princess Isabel of Portugal, the duke's fiancée. A later source also refers to a map of the world that Jan supposedly produced for his employer.

Shortly after his appointment in 1425, Jan travelled to Lille – the duke's preferred residence. In the ensuing years, he was sent on a number of secret diplomatic missions. Van Eyck was, for instance, part of the delegation that journeyed to Portugal to negotiate Philip's marriage to the Infanta Isabel.

He settled permanently in Bruges in 1430. All the paintings that can be firmly attributed to him date from his Bruges period. They were generally portraits (such as the *Portrait of Margareta van Eyck*) and small religious paintings, which he produced for prominent citizens of Bruges and other wealthy patrons. He self-confidently signed and dated his works – which was not customary at the time – and sometimes added his motto 'als ich can' ('to the best of my ability').

The first and largest surviving painting by Van Eyck is the *Adoration of the Lamb*, the so-called *Ghent Altarpiece* (finished 1432), in St Bavo's Cathedral, Ghent. According to the inscription, Jan's brother Hubrecht also worked on the painting. His contribution remains unclear, however, as no other paintings by him are known. The second-largest painting in Jan's oeuvre is the *Virgin and Child with Canon Joris van der Paele* (1436).

Van Eyck remained in Philip the Good's service for the rest of his life. He died in Bruges in 1441 and was buried in the Church of St Donatian, which was demolished in 1799.

His highly innovatory style is rooted in late-medieval miniature art, which combined naturalism with decoration. The religious symbolism of his compositions suggests great learning, while his interest in people and nature points towards a humanist mentality. He was a characteristic personality of the New Era that was shortly to dawn. Van Eyck proved a vital link in the development of European painting, not least through his influence on all the great Flemish artists of the 15th and early 16th centuries.

The Virgin and Child with Canon Joris van der Paele, detail

The Flemish Primitives

The term 'Flemish Primitives' was coined in the 19th century to describe the school of painting that flourished in the 15th century in a number of towns in the Southern Netherlands, most notably Bruges, Ghent, Tournai, Brussels, Louvain and 's-Hertogenbosch (Bois-le-Duc). The region belonged to the realm of the Dukes of Burgundy and was Europe's economic centre at the time. The patronage of the court, upper middle class and the Church created the ideal conditions for the vigorous development of artistic life.

The art of the Flemish Primitives was viewed simultaneously as an offshoot of the late-Gothic style and the beginning of the Renaissance in northern painting. Its features include a heightened attention to landscape, people and everyday life, the skilful rendering of detail and profuse symbolism – often disguised. Having perfected the technique of oil painting, these artists were able to achieve an unprecedented realism in their rendition of the physical world. This realism was accompanied by a religious interpretation of the cosmos as God's creation, embracing both heaven and earth. This highly sophisticated art was labelled 'primitive' in the 19th century on the grounds that it preceded the classical art of the Renaissance and the later academic schools and especially because it did not yet apply the principles of linear perspective.

The founders of the new style were the Master of Flémalle in Tournai, Jan van Eyck in Bruges and Rogier van der Weyden in Brussels. Its technical and spiritual riches were then developed in the second half of the 15th century by five outstanding figures, each of whom added his own vision. They were Petrus Christus, Hans Memling and Gerard David in Bruges, Dieric Bouts in Louvain and Hugo van der Goes in Ghent. With the exception of Bouts (by whom there is an important painting in Holy Saviour's Cathedral in Bruges) all these masters are represented in the Groeninge Museum.

Petrus Christus, *Isabel of Portugal with St Elizabeth*, c. 1457–60, panel, 59 x 33 cm, left wing of a triptych

Little is known about Jan van Eyck's wife. She was called Margareta, was substantially younger than her husband and outlived him by at least fifteen years. She bore him two children. The Latin text on the original frame is painted to resemble an inscription carved in stone. It reads: 'my husband Johannes completed me in the year 1439 on 17 June – I was 33 years old at the time – als ich can.' Van Eyck used his motto *als ich can* ('to the best of my ability') as his signature. It might embody a reference to his name (ich/Eyck).

The subjects of Van Eyck's portraits are always turned a little to the left – a position that adds depth to the figure. Margareta is shown sitting three-quarters to the left, turned towards the light source – a window reflected in her eyes – and looks directly at the artist and hence the viewer. She wears a ring on her right ring-finger, which we can just make out above the bottom of the frame. Her hair is worn high in the fashionable horn-style, held in place by a checkerboard hairnet. The white highlights of the flounced headdress, the dark background and the deep red of the bodice create a sober harmony in keeping with Margareta's composed expression – her features softened by the ghost of a smile.

Virgin and Child late 15th century

Copy after the Master of Flémalle
first half 15th century
Panel, 43 x 30.5 cm

Favourite compositions by leading masters were frequently copied in the 15th century. The copies could be partial or complete. Some were painted by the artist himself or his assistants (replicas), while others were done by contemporaries or later followers. When the original painting has failed to survive down the centuries – which is all too often the case – art historians are naturally thrilled to come across a carefully executed copy.

This *Virgin and Child* is a copy after a lost composition by the Master of Flémalle – a key figure in art-historical terms. The original work was painted in the first half of the 15th century and the copy towards its close. The gold-brocade cushion on which the Madonna rests her arms and, probably, the cloth in the background are inventions of the copyist, who convincingly succeeded in adopting the Master of Flémalle's style, even if the result is slightly stiff.

The Virgin and Child theme was extremely common in late-medieval art. The Child often holds a piece of fruit in his hand to symbolise his redemption of the sin committed by Adam and Eve. The Southern Netherlandish masters of the 15th century do not present the Mother of God as an inaccessible or majestic figure, but as an idealised human being in tender contact with her baby.

The enigmatic Master of Flémalle, who was active in Tournai between roughly 1410–15 and 1440, was one of the earliest Flemish Primitives. Even before Jan van Eyck, he abandoned the stylised 'International Gothic' manner and developed a realistic style based on the new oil-painting technique and an exceptional skill in the rendering of matter, light and volume. The Master of Flémalle is often identified as the Tournai artist Robert Campin.

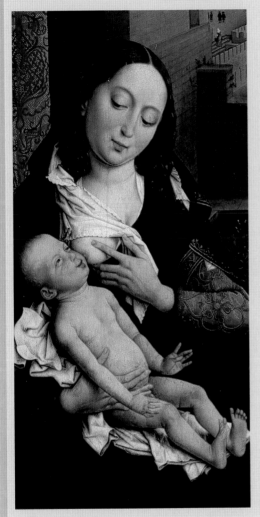

St Luke Drawing the Virgin's Portrait. Rogier settled in Brussels around 1435, where he was appointed municipal painter. It was at this time that he adopted the Flemish version of his name, Rogier van der Weyden. In addition to the City Council, he received commissions from civil institutions and the Church, and also from the Burgundian court. He achieved eternal fame with a series of altarpieces, which present the Passion of Christ in a dramatic yet restrained manner. His emotional and sacred style had a profound influence on art in the Low Countries and beyond. Van der Weyden's reputation also rests on a number of portraits of the Burgundian nobility and Flemish bourgeoisie. He died in Brussels in 1464.

The presence in the Groeninge Museum of a key work by Jan van Eyck (see pp. 8–9) and an excellent copy of an important Van der Weyden composition (see pp. 18–19) provides us with the opportunity to compare Rogier's style with that of his slightly older contemporary. Van Eyck has discovered the physical world and nature, yet his figures seem emotionally static and their movements frozen. A contemplative, liturgical mood hangs over his images. Van der Weyden adopts Van Eyck's focus on the spatial surroundings, but gives his human figures greater depth and emotion. They are expressive and make supple gestures. The space in which they move is, however, restricted to the central area, which is clearly separated from the background. Whereas Van Eyck presents people in unity with the earthly and heavenly spheres, Van der Weyden is chiefly concerned with their mood and emotional expression.

Rogier van der Weyden was the direct successor to the style of the Master of Flémalle (Robert Campin). He was born Rogier de le Pasture in Tournai around 1399 and worked in Robert Campin's workshop from 1427 to 1432. He became a free master painter in 1432. Van der Weyden rapidly fell under the influence of Jan van Eyck too, as we see in his early work

St Luke Drawing the Virgin's Portrait, detail

St Luke Drawing the Virgin's Portrait c. 1500

Copy after Rogier van der Weyden
c. 1399–1464
Panel, 133 x 107 cm

Luke was one of the four gospel-writers, who recounted the life of Christ. According to an early-medieval legend, he once drew or painted a portrait of the Virgin Mary. The story may have arisen from the fact that Luke wrote in greater detail than the other three Evangelists about Christ's mother. Whatever the case, he was soon adopted as the patron saint of painters, whose guilds and corporations often chose an image of Luke painting the Virgin's portrait to decorate their altars.

Rogier van der Weyden's *St Luke Drawing the Virgin's Portrait* is one of the loveliest treatments of the theme. He painted it around 1434 and it may now be seen in Boston's Museum of Fine Arts. The panel in the Groeninge Museum is an expertly painted, full-size copy, which was produced towards the end of the 15th century.

The scene is set in a bourgeois interior with a very human feel – there are no haloes or other divine attributes to point out the holy nature of the depicted figures. St Luke's customary attributes, a copy of his gospel and the bull, have been pushed into the back-ground. They appear in the study, a corner of which we glimpse on the right. Mary feeds her baby in a room resembling a portico. It opens onto an enclosed garden, beyond which we see a section of the city walls, the city itself and a landscape divided by a river. The Virgin sits humbly on the step of her wooden throne, with its decorative canopy. Luke is busy drawing her portrait in silverpoint on a sheet of paper or parchment resting on a piece of wood.

Van der Weyden drew inspiration for the landscape and the interior from a panel that Jan van Eyck painted in the same period (c. 1434), the *Virgin and Child with Chancellor Rolin* (Musée du Louvre, Paris). The human figures, by contrast, display his personal and expressive style: Jesus is a lively little boy, Mary beams with maternal joy and Luke concentrates entirely on his task.

The Annunciation, The Nativity 1452   Petrus Christus *c.* 1420–1475/76
Panels, each 88.5 x 54.8 cm
Probably fragments of a polyptych

Petrus Christus was fascinated by the construction of space in the two-dimensional picture plane. This interest is evident in these panels, the actual themes of which attract less attention than their carefully worked-out setting. Christus explored the possibilities of representing depth and was the first Netherlandish artist to apply central perspective on a systematic basis. In his *Annunciation*, he placed the vanishing point at which virtually all the perspective lines converge on the tip of the Archangel Gabriel's staff.

His painting style is also marked by its rich colours and heavy shadows. The figures are round and doll-like, and their expressions cool. The subdued atmosphere, refined finish and sense of detail recall Van Eyck's paintings.

We know little about Petrus Christus. He probably came from the village of Baarle, to the south-east of Breda. In 1444, he purchased citizenship of Bruges, a flourishing commercial and political centre where artists could find attractive commissions. He duly became successful and achieved a high social status, no doubt assisted by his stylistic similarity to Jan van Eyck, who had died in 1441. Petrus Christus himself died in Bruges in 1475 or 1476.

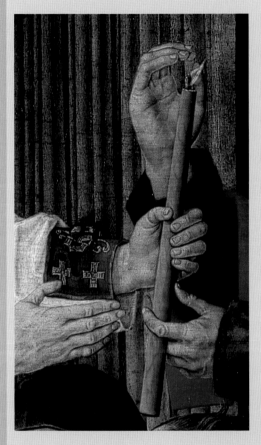

Death of the Virgin, detail

We know virtually nothing about the first half of Hugo van der Goes' life. He appears to have been born around 1442 in Ghent, where he enrolled as a master in the painters' guild in 1467. Hugo worked in the city for ten years, receiving prestigious commissions from the City Council, churches and monasteries, and the Burgundian court. It was during this period that he painted his masterpiece, the *Portinari Triptych* (Galleria degli Uffizi, Florence), the centre panel of which contains his famous Adoration of the Shepherds. In 1477, at the height of his career as a painter, he moved to Rouge-Cloître in the Forest of Soignes near Brussels, where he became a kind of lay brother, though he continued to accept commissions. He suffered from bouts of depression, which eventually culminated in a mental breakdown in 1481. Following his convalescence, he resumed work as a painter and lay brother. It was during this final stage of his life that he is said to have painted his *Death of the Virgin*. Hugo never signed or dated his panels, however, which has made it very difficult to date his work. He died in 1482–83.

Like Jan van Eyck and Rogier van der Weyden, Hugo van der Goes was an isolated phenomenon. And like them, he was to influence many generations of artists. He developed the dimension of movement in painting – not the suggestion of movement in a gesture or pose, but as a fundamental element of the entire composition. This dynamic aspect conveys an emotional, visionary and religious nature. The expressive and realistic rendering of the figures, with a marked preference for ordinary faces and strong hands, is another characteristic of Van der Goes' painting. More than five hundred years later, the humanity of his images continues to grip the viewer.

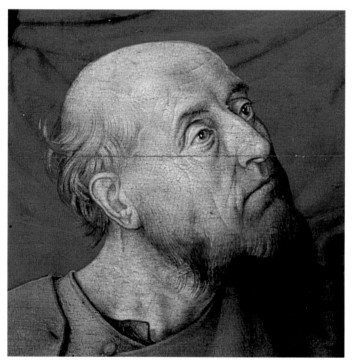

The *Death of the Virgin* might well have been the final work that Hugo van der Goes completed. He probably painted it for Ter Duinen Abbey in Koksijde.

The artist interprets the theme in a very personal way. The vision of heaven above Mary's deathbed, the unearthly colours in the soft, blue light and the enclosed space give this image of the emotional group of apostles a sense of unreality, as if we were witnessing a dream or delusion. The figures are filled with sorrow and the sense of despair is heightened by the movement of many hands. The painting includes few precious materials or picturesque elements. Van der Goes eschews such details in order to concentrate entirely on the emotion and on the supernatural world. The shades of light in the drapery of the robes and the gleaming highlights of the skin are seemingly generated by the heavenly glow in the upper left part of the painting. The sharply delineated, graphic handling of the faces, hands and feet lends clarity to an agitated scene. The composition is structured by the prominent tonalities of the fabrics.

Hugo van der Goes was the most 'modern' of the Flemish Primitives – a fact that is plainly evident in this *Death of the Virgin* from such features as the realistic and expressive rendering of the figures and the movement and heightened emotion that permeate the composition. The mystical, religious spirit allied to a strong sense of emotion – features that differ markedly from the impassive devotion we find in, say, Petrus Christus – make this intriguing panel one of the masterpieces of 15th-century painting.

Triptych of Willem Moreel 1484

Hans Memling c. 1440–1494
Panel, 121.1 x 153.4 cm (centre panel),
120.7 x 69 cm and 121 x 68.6 cm (wings)
Altarpiece for the altar of SS Maurus and Giles in the Church of St James
in Bruges
(wings) *Willem Moreel with his sons and patron saint* (left) and
Barbara van Vlaenderberch with her daughters and patron saint
(closed wings) *St John* (left) and *St George*

Several tall and handsome figures stand serenely and almost motionlessly in a landscape. On either side of them, we see the donors of the painting kneeling piously with their children. Despite the detailed rendering of the figures and the surrounding space, the image does not feel like an image of reality. What we see is a scene from paradise with divine figures and blessed human beings, entirely free of fear and passion. Everything is perfect in this dreamworld, in which the holy and the human flow together without the slightest ripple.

The *Moreel Triptych* represents the essence of Memling's art. It was painted in 1484 for Willem Moreel, a prominent Bruges politician, and his wife Barbara van Vlaenderberch *née* van Hertsvelde. The painting was destined for the Church of St James in Bruges, where the couple wished eventually to be buried. They installed an altar close to their future burial place with the triptych as its altarpiece. This background helps explain the nature of the image.

At the centre of the triptych we see the giant Christopher who,

according to medieval legend, carried the Christ Child across a river on his shoulders. His way is lit by the hermit we make out in the distance. Christopher was invoked against sudden death, which made him a suitable figure for a triptych destined for a private mausoleum.

The two other saints do not belong in the legend of St Christopher but were placed in the same landscape – if somewhat separated by the rocks – in order to maintain the unity of the composition. To the left we see the former monk St Maurus, with his crook and open

book, and to the right St Giles, a Benedictine hermit with an arrow in his arm and a deer at his side. The presence of Maurus and Giles relates to the donors' surnames: 'Moreel' is linked etymologically with 'Moor' or *Maurus* in Latin, while the name 'Hertsvelde' reflects a detail from the legend of St Giles (*hert* is Dutch for 'deer').

The magnificent landscape continues into the open wings. Here we see the donors kneeling with their children and their respective patron saints, William and Barbara. In other words, both the first names and surnames of Willem Moreel and his wife are linked in this painting to patron saints. St John and St George, who are painted in monochrome brown (grisaille) on the reverses of the wings were the patron saints of two of Moreel's sons.

The triptych as a whole is a brilliant illustration of Hans Memling's religious art and his talent as a portrait painter. This is, moreover, the earliest portrait of a whole, large family in the Low Countries.

Hans Memling was a master of the idealised, realistic portrait. Looking at the donors' family in this triptych, it is easy to understand why so many rich Bruges burghers were keen to have him paint their portraits. The Moreels' social status is radiated not only by their refined expressions, but also from their clothes – from which, incidentally, we can get an idea of contemporary *haute couture*. Over his black jerkin, Willem wears a fashionable item from the 1480s – a fur-lined tabard, with no fastenings or belt. Barbara is dressed just as modiously in a dress of black damask silk, with a separate white collar and a wide girdle with a gold buckle. Several of her daughters wear a *frontelle* on their forehead – a black loop attached to a cap or fillet. Contemporary fashion also dictated features like the low-cut bodices worn over camisoles or fine, collarless blouses, and the tightly swept-back hair, with caps worn at the back of the head and a long, translucent veil.

The first historical reference to Hans Memling is his registration as a citizen of Bruges on 30 January 1465. The Citizens Register lists him as 'Jan van Mimnelinghe', from the town of Seligenstadt on the river Main in Germany. As time passed, he evidently used the name 'Hans Memling', as Bruges documents refer to him as 'Master Hans' and he signed two of his works with the name 'Memling'.

He is believed to have arrived in Bruges at the age of about 25, having worked for a while in the Brussels workshop run by Rogier van der Weyden. He soon began to receive important commissions. Fifteen years later, he had become one of the city's richest citizens. He lived with his wife Tanne and their three children in a large stone house in Sint-Jorisstraat, 'over the Vlaming [Fleming] Bridge'. At the height of his painter's career, in the 1480s, he probably employed a number of assistants, who will have helped him to paint the *Moreel Triptych*, preparing the panel and perhaps adding 'staffage' to the landscape.

The vast majority of Memling's patrons were wealthy burghers – bankers, merchants, politicians – and clergymen. He also received one or two commissions from nobles but, unlike his contemporary Hugo van der Goes, he never worked for the Dukes of Burgundy. Memling was very much the painter of Bruges' bourgeoisie and the city's foreign elite. He died in Bruges in 1494.

Memling's painting style proved highly influential and was still being imitated in Bruges a hundred years later. On the one hand, his idealised images evoke the mystic, Christian spirit of the late Middle Ages, while on the other, his art has come to symbolise Bruges' prosperity in the Burgundian era. Memling actually witnessed the end of that era, which occurred in 1477 when Mary of Burgundy married Maximilian of Austria. Their wedding marked the moment at which the Burgundian dynasty was absorbed into that of the Habsburgs.

Bruges' medieval past continues to appeal to the imagination. You can rediscover it not only in the paintings of the Flemish Primitives, but also in the many historic buildings and picturesque corners of the old city.

Reverse of a pair of wings showing the *Annunciation, c.* 1467–70, panels, each 83.3 x 26.5 cm. These 'semi-grisailles' – the figures are presented as statues in a niche, but are not treated as sculptures – originally belonged to a Crucifixion triptych *(Triptych of Jan Crabbe)*. The centre panel is now in the Museo Civico in Vicenza, while the insides of the wings (which were separated from the outsides) are in the Pierpont Morgan Library, New York

The Judgement of Cambyses 1498

Gerard David c. 1460–1523
Panel, 182.3 x 159.2 cm (left panel)
and 182.2 x 159.4 cm
Justice diptych for the Council
Chamber of Bruges Town Hall

This is a gruesome scene that might well be labelled 'not suitable for sensitive viewers'. What on earth did the unfortunate wretch do to deserve such a horrific fate? And why is his torture depicted with such unbearable detail and on such a large scale?

According to an old Persian story, Sisamnes was a corrupt judge who was skinned alive on the orders of King Cambyses. The judicial throne from which Otanes, Sisamnes' son and successor, was henceforth to dispense justice was to be covered with the skin. The left-hand panel of the diptych shows Sisamnes' arrest in the presence of Cambyses, who is summing up the charges against him. One of the judge's crimes was to accept a bribe in return for delivering a false judgement. We see him in the background in the porch of his house receiving a purse. In the upper right part of the other panel, which shows the flaying of Sisamnes, Otanes sits in judgement on the throne covered with his father's skin.

The panels were originally connected and hung as a 'justice scene' in the Council Chamber of Bruges Town Hall. Aldermen also had a judicial role at the time and so the chamber could also function as a court. The purpose of the painting was to serve as a permanent reminder to the aldermen of their duty of impartiality as judges. The public location for which it was painted explains the large size of the work and also why the coats of arms of Philip the Fair and Joan of Aragon (who then ruled the Netherlands)

feature in the 'arrest' panel and those of Flanders and Bruges on the side with the 'flaying'.

The artist places the entire episode in a Flemish city with Gothic buildings. He includes a

number of unusual features in the architecture, below a portico with porphyry columns and Corinthian capitals: antique medallions, garlands of flowers and *putti* – ultramodern ornaments, in other words,

Gerard David offered a final, brilliant synthesis of the technical and spiritual tradition of the century of Van Eyck. However, his development of volume, his focus on naturalistic effects and his use of Renaissance decorative motifs also made him a herald of the 16th century.

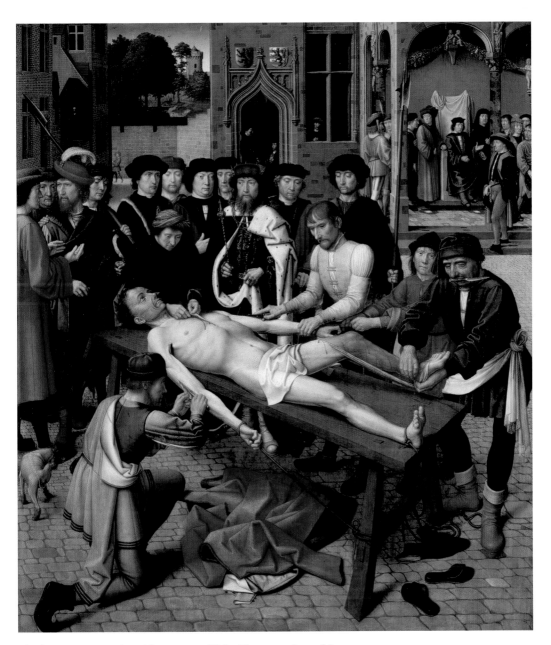

of Italian origin. Gerard David was one of the first Netherlandish artists to incorporate Renaissance motifs in his paintings. The bright, rich colours are also striking, as is the brilliant treatment of volume, space and light. The atmosphere of the scene is distant and affectless. Although typical of Gerard David's style, its combination with this horrifying scene sends genuine shivers down the spine.

GERARD DAVID

The last great Flemish Primitive artist was the Dutchman
Gerard David. He was born in Oudewater in Holland around
1460, and probably received his training in his native town
and subsequently in Haarlem. He was evidently living in
Bruges by 1484, when he was admitted into the painters' corporation. The late 15th century was not the best time to come
and work in Bruges. The good times had well and truly gone.
The unexpected death of Duke Charles the Bold in battle near
Nancy in 1477 plunged the Burgundian Netherlands into a
period of political uncertainty and social unrest. A series of
urban revolts and wars put a damper on artistic life. Despite
Bruges' artistic decline, Gerard David managed to run a successful workshop there for forty years. He was well connected and was able to marry the daughter of a wealthy gold-
smith. His commissions came from prominent churchmen
and the municipal authorities. David took over Memling's
leading role following the latter's death in 1494. Gerard
David himself died in Bruges in 1523.

David's work expresses the spirit that prevailed around
1500, when new ideas began to seep in among the deep roots
of Flemish tradition. On the one hand, he was influenced by
the great 15th-century masters, as we can plainly see in his
Baptism of Christ. The precision, realism and smooth technique are all reminiscent of Van Eyck, Van der Goes and
Memling. On the other hand, he was receptive to the great
artistic renewal coming out of Italy. His *Judgement of
Cambyses* is one of the earliest Flemish paintings to feature
Renaissance elements like festoons and *putti*.

The Baptism of Christ, detail of centre panel

The Baptism of Christ, reverses of the wings

The Baptism of Christ early 16th century   Gerard David c. 1460–1523
Panel, 129.7 x 96.6 cm (centre panel), 132 x 43.1 cm and 132.2 x 42.2 cm (wings)
Triptych from the altar of the Tribunal at the Church of St Basil in Bruges
(from 1520)
(wings) *Jan des Trompes with his son and patron saint* (left)
and *Elisabeth van der Meersch with her daughters and patron saint*
(closed wings) *Virgin and Child* (left) and *Magdalena Cordier with her daughter
and patron saint*

The Baptism of Christ by the prophet John is set in a fascinating, imaginary landscape that runs across all three panels. Jesus stands in the river Jordan. The Holy Ghost hovers directly above him in the form of a dove, with God the Father higher still, just as the gospels recount. The angel holding Jesus' robe is an addition by the artist. Other episodes from the life of John the Baptist are depicted in the background: on the left, we see him preaching, while on the right he is shown presenting Jesus to a group of people with the words 'Here is the Lamb of God'. The fortified city on the distant hill is probably meant to represent the Heavenly Jerusalem.

The painting dates from a few years after the Justice diptych but in artistic terms, it represents a step back into the past. The figures resemble those of Memling, standing apart from one another, emotionless and immobile, while the landscape breathes the silent, almost vacuum-like atmosphere that is so characteristic of the Flemish Primitives.

Despite the debt he owed to his predecessors, Gerard David developed a personal style with a number of striking characteristics. The colouring is deep and full – even somewhat intense – while the landscape is executed with immense refinement. The artist has also taken care to render the scenes correctly using various types of perspective. The mood of his paintings is cool, with graceful but serious figures that gaze fixedly into the distance.

The triptych was commissioned by Jan des Trompes, a prominent Bruges civil servant, who is portrayed with his first wife and their children in the open wings of the triptych. As usual, they are accompanied by their patron saints, John and Elizabeth. The reverses of the wings show a Virgin and Child opposite des Trompes' second wife, their first daughter and Mary Magdalene.

Ursula was a pious princess, whom a heathen prince asked to become his wife. She promised that she would marry him provided that he converted to Christianity and allowed her to make a pilgrimage to Rome, accompanied by eleven thousand virgins. Her suitor agreed and Ursula and her enormous company were duly received by the Pope in Rome. During the return journey, they were captured in Cologne by Guam, King of the Huns, who murdered Ursula, her betrothed Eutherius, the eleven thousand virgins, and the Pope and his retinue, who had travelled back with them.

The eight panels, the name piece of the anonymous Master of the Ursula Legend, bring the medieval legend to life in the manner of a cartoon strip. The left wing (not shown here) contains the following scenes: a letter is delivered containing the proposal of marriage; the embarkation of the virgins; Ursula bids farewell to her parents; an angel appears to her in Cologne with a warning.

The two small wings depicting the Church and the Synagogue probably came from the same altarpiece.

The company leaves Basle on foot for Rome, where the Pope waits in the distance

Ursula leaves Rome with Pope Cyriacus and his retinue

Ursula and her companions are murdered in Cologne

Worshippers venerate relics of Ursula and the eleven thousand virgins

St Nicholas c. 1486–93

Master of the Lucy Legend,
late 15th and early 16th century
Panel, 101.5 x 81.5 cm
Centre panel of a triptych

We know that this figure giving his blessing is St Nicholas because the wings, now in a private collection, show miracles from the legend of this bishop and children's friend. The triptych is attributed to the Master of the Lucy Legend, whose style can be readily recognised. The backgrounds to his paintings, for instance, often contain views of Bruges, with precisely rendered towers. The artist also displayed a fascination for precious stones and expensive fabrics. He was somewhat weaker, however, when it came to facial features and hands. The figure of St Nicholas is rather stiff and lacks expression.

The fine panorama of Bruges is the most noteworthy aspect of this panel. All the towers that it includes can still be seen (albeit somewhat modified) as you walk around the city. From left to right, they belong to the Church of Our Lady, Holy Saviour's, the Oosterlingenhuis (former base of the Hanseatic merchants), the Belfry, the Poorters (Citizen's) Lodge and, to the right of the canopy, the Jerusalem Church.

A number of minor masters, many of whom remain anonymous, were active in the shadow of the leading Flemish Primitives. They developed their own, in some cases rather naïve style. Although they lacked the cosmic vision, originality or emotional impact of the great painters, they still produced fascinating and high-quality work.

The Adoration of the Shepherds,
The Adoration of the Magi first quarter 16th century
Anonymous Bruges master
Panels, each 91 x 59 cm
Wings of a triptych
(reverse) *The Miracle of the flowing oil*

The left-hand panel showing the *Adoration of the Shepherds* is a night scene, which was fairly unusual in Bruges art around the beginning of the 16th century. The anonymous Bruges master took the idea of a nocturnal scene with the Christ Child as the source of the light from a painting by Hugo van der Goes, while the composition and figures were copied from Gerard David. The other panel, showing the *Adoration of the Magi*, was also inspired by Hugo van der Goes, while the halberdier with the red cap and the man with the white turban were lifted directly from a print by Albrecht Dürer.

The reverse of the panels contains the biblical story of the prophet Elisha and the widow. The latter had fallen deeply into debt and begged Elisha to help her. Elisha performed a miracle – the last few drops of oil the widow possessed continued to flow until she had filled several barrels. The money they raised was then sufficient to pay off her creditors.

The two Adoration scenes illustrate how strongly Bruges artists

continued to elaborate on the local tradition in the early part of the 16th century, while their counterparts in cities like Antwerp and Brussels were adopting a style that moved away from the typically pious atmosphere of the 15th century towards more human and lively scenes, decorated with ornamental Italian motifs. These Bruges panels have a touch of that development. The architectural setting in which the kings come to offer their gifts and – albeit through the echoes of Van der Goes – the dynamic scene with the horses in the background, the nocturnal mood and remarkable lighting in the stable with the shepherds, and the debt to Dürer all point cautiously in the modern direction.

Hieronymus Bosch (attributed to) *c*. 1450–1516
Panel, 99.5 x 60.3 cm (centre panel), 99.5 x 28.8 cm
and 99.5 x 28.5 cm (wings)
(wings) *Heaven* (left) and *Hell*
(closed wings) *Christ Crowned with Thorns* (grisaille)

The triptych shows the three main
elements of Judgement Day, following a scheme that had been developed by medieval Christian
thought. The Last Judgement takes
place in the middle, where Christ
appears in the firmament to judge
all human beings: the blessed souls
are directed towards heaven and the
damned towards hell.

The style of Hieronymus Bosch
is clearly recognisable in the small
figures, the strange and monstrous
elements, the colours and the fine,
transparent painting technique.
Bosch's images are rooted in
medieval fantasy and symbolism
– a legacy from which he developed
a pictorial idiom packed with intriguing ideas, and with the same
philosophical and moralising tone
as the literature of the time. A recur-
ring theme in Bosch is the rise of
evil and stupidity, which, in the
form of monsters and demons,
threaten beauty and the light. This
pessimistic vision may have been
influenced by the spirit of the times.
The end of the Middle Ages was a
transitional period marked by economic malaise, uncertainty and
social confusion.

Bosch remains a unique phenomenon in art history, although
his work has been widely plagiar-
ised. A number of experts consider
this *Last Judgement* to be an excellent early 16th-century imitation of
his work.

Hieronymus Bosch, or Hieronymus van Aken, was born in 's-Hertogenbosch in the duchy of Brabant (now in the Netherlands). We do
not know a great deal more about him than that he spent his entire
painter's career there, as his father and grandfather had done before
him, and that he grew rich and famous. He died in his native city. His
best-known work is the *Garden of Earthly Delights* (Prado, Madrid).

The inscription in gold letters states the date and place of the painting's execution, the name and age of the subject and Christ's monogram at the top, but not the name of the artist. The portrait has, however, been firmly attributed to the Bruges painter Adriaan Isenbrant on the basis of stylistic analysis.

The subject is the Genoese businessman Paulus de Nigro, who is shown at the age of 36. He worked in insurance, providing cover for ships and their cargoes in Bruges and Antwerp. It is evident from his black jerkin with its fur collar that he was a figure of some importance. He is soberly dressed, though he wears several unobtrusive jewels, including a ring with his initials. The man is shown in three-quarter view, turned towards the right. His prayerful pose suggests that there was a pendant panel, possibly showing a Virgin and Child. However, diptychs with the donor on the left and a religious theme on the right were not usual at the time, from which art historians have concluded that the panel belonged to a triptych, with Paulus de Nigro on the left, the Virgin Mary in the middle and the donor's wife or another relative in the right wing.

There are no sharp outlines in this painting. Shapes seem to merge into one another, while the facial features are rendered in a soft and diffuse manner. The nuances of the skin colour were achieved using the technique of thin, transparent layers of paint. The dark-green background, the black hair and the black beret make the overall colouring fairly sombre, but this lends the portrait a powerful expression, despite its small size.

The Virgin and Child with St Catherine and St Barbara c. 1520–25

Master of the Holy Blood, first quarter 16th century
Panel, 87.5 x 66 cm (centre panel), 88.5 x 28 cm (wings)
(wings) *Joachim Christiaens and his patron saint* (left) and
Jossine Lamsins and her patron saint Judocus
(closed wings) *Annunciation* (grisaille)

The Virgin Mary sits with the Christ Child and the martyrs St Catherine and St Barbara in a landscape that continues across all three panels. The knapsack that Joseph carries over his shoulder (background, right) suggests that this is an image of the Flight into Egypt, although Barbara and Catherine have nothing to do with that story. Barbara is shown holding a peacock feather and her book, but lacks her most important attribute – the tower in which she was imprisoned by her heathen father. Catherine can be identified by her 'mystic marriage' to Christ, which she saw in a vision: the Child puts a ring on her finger.

She too is missing her key attribute – the wheel on which she was to be put to death, only for her to be saved by an angel. Perhaps the round diadem she wears is intended to represent the instrument of her torture. The sword with which she was eventually beheaded appears behind her.

The altarpiece was commissioned by Jan van Cattenbrouck and his wife Jossine Lamsins. Jossine remarried following Jan's death and she had the portrait of her first husband and his patron saint, John the Baptist, overpainted with the features of her second husband, whose patron saint was Joachim. Several of

the changes left traces that can be made out by the naked eye. The lamb in St Joachim's arms, for instance, is a later addition, through which the cloak and book can be seen. Joachim Christiaens' coat of arms on the prie-dieu also reveals the changes that were made.

The Master of the Holy Blood was a follower of Hans Memling and Gerard David. The name by which he is known to art historians is derived from his *Lamentation Triptych* in the Museum of the Noble Confraternity of the Holy Blood in Bruges. There is another important work by this artist in the Church of St James.

The Rest on the Flight into Egypt second quarter 16th century
Ambrosius Benson c. 1499–1550
Panel, 103 x 65 cm
Centre panel of a triptych

This scene comes from an episode in the Gospel according to Matthew. An angel appeared to Joseph, Jesus' foster-father, in a dream and told him to flee: 'Then Joseph got up, took the child and his mother by night, and went to Egypt.' In the first centuries AD, a number of legends grew up around the episode, several of which are depicted in this painting.

While Mary suckles her baby, Joseph is seen in the background giving the donkey water. Two legendary episodes appear further back in the landscape: the Miracle of the Corn and the Casting Down of the Idols. The Holy Family passed a field in which a farmer was sowing seed. When Herod's soldiers reached the spot, the corn had miraculously grown and ripened. The farmer was able to say truthfully that he had seen the fleeing family when sowing his corn. The soldiers assumed it must have been months earlier and gave up their pursuit. Another legend tells how images of pagan gods fell spontaneously to the ground as Jesus and his mother approached. The barren tree might be intended as a symbol of heathendom, contrasting with the flourishing wood on the right.

The hinges that are still attached to the frame tell us that this painting was the centre panel of a triptych, the wings of which have been lost.

It seems that anything goes in art. Take the touchingly naïve detail showing a Flemish village church with its belltower in a landscape supposedly representing the road to Egypt, along which Mary, Joseph and the newborn Jesus fled the Holy Land

Mary Magdalene second quarter 16th century
Ambrosius Benson *c.* 1499–1550
Panel, 69.5 x 55.5 cm

The chiaroscuro technique, whereby the dark reds and greens contrast sharply with the ivory-coloured and heavily shadowed skin, is also very Southern European. Benson's own style is recognisable in features like the hands, with their long, slender fingers, and the precisely painted and highlighted wrinkles of the sleeves – all characteristics that are also apparent in his *Rest on the Flight into Egypt.*

By excluding superfluous details, the artist gives Mary Magdalene a classical, serene and even monumental presence. The Renaissance came to Bruges somewhat later than it did to Antwerp and Brussels.

Ambrosius Benson was born in Lombardy (northern Italy). He emigrated to Flanders as a young painter, ending up in Bruges. He initially lived and worked with Gerard David, but set up as an independent master after falling out with his boss. Before long, he rose to a high position in the painters' guild. Like most of his colleagues in Bruges, he painted both religious works and portraits. Benson focused successfully on the international market. Two of his sons also went on to become professional painters.

That Benson truly was a transitional figure between the Middle Ages and the Early Modern Era, between North and South, and between the Flemish Primitives and the Renaissance is plain if we compare this *Mary Magdalene* with the painter's *Rest on the Flight into Egypt.* The latter is still very traditional and Flemish, while this image of the Magdalene has a modern and Italian feel.

The classical face and the brownish *sfumato* of the modelling are reminiscent of Raphael (1483–1520) and Leonardo da Vinci (1452–1519).

The scene depicted in this magnificent panorama is Christ's wounding
with the lance. According to tradition, the blind Roman centurion
Longinus pierced the crucified
Jesus' side with his lance. A drop of
blood ran down and splashed into
his eye, immediately restoring his
sight. Meanwhile, darkness fell over
the land, the temple curtain was
torn in two, the earth shook and the
graves opened. According to
Matthew's Gospel: 'Now when the
centurion and those with him, who
were keeping watch over Jesus, saw
the earthquake and what took place,
they were terrified and said, "Truly
this man was God's Son!"' The centurion in the painting could be
speaking these words just as his
eyes were 'opened'. The moment is
dramatic and is evoked with a great
deal of realism. This is an unusual
composition, in spite of the use of
traditional elements, such as the figure of the Magdalene embracing the
cross, the grieving group on the left
and the soldiers playing dice and
squabbling on the right. The long,
unruly procession of soldiers
returning to Jerusalem links up
with the scene in the foreground to
form a single, meandering ensemble
that begins on the left with St John
and the Virgin. The effect is that of
the journey to Calvary in reverse.

Jerusalem is rendered in the left
background with a profusion of
topographical details that testify to
the fact that Provoost had visited the
city in person. The large number of
horses shown from every possible
angle, the lances that point aggres-
sively into the air and many other
elements turn the painting into an
almost inexhaustible spectacle.

Although the leading Renaissance painter in the Low Countries was Quentin Massys in Antwerp, Jan Provoost was certainly one of the school's most important representatives. He was born in Mons, trained in Valenciennes and then moved to Antwerp, where he enrolled in the Guild of St Luke – the painters' professional organisation – in 1493. During his time in the city, he came under the influence of Quentin Massys. He purchased citizenship of Bruges in 1494, the year in which Hans Memling died, leaving Gerard David to perpetuate the great Flemish pictorial tradition.

Provoost's innovative style brought new life to painting in Bruges. He made a pilgrimage to the Holy Land some time around 1500, which also enabled him to visit Italy. He painted his *Crucifixion* shortly afterwards. Provoost received a variety of commissions between 1509 and 1527 from the Church, the City Council *(The Last Judgement)* and other political institutions. Like his colleagues, he also worked for private citizens who liked to have their portraits painted in the wings of a triptych featuring a religious theme *(Donor with St Nicholas* and *Donor's Wife with St Godeliva)*.

Provoost oversaw the decoration of the city to mark the

Joyful Entry of Charles V into Bruges in 1520. The project entailed close collaboration with the local 'rederijkers' – those keen practitioners of rhetoric who were responsible for the content of the festivities, the dramatic performances and tableaux vivants. Some of Provoost's complex and literary paintings, including his *Death and the Miser*, may have been inspired by such encounters.

The artist probably kept up a workshop in both Antwerp and Bruges. It was in Antwerp in 1520 that he met the great German Renaissance artist Albrecht Dürer, whom he then accompanied to Bruges. During this period Antwerp evolved into the most important commercial centre in the Low Countries and also came to overshadow once-dazzling Bruges in the artistic stakes. Jan Provoost died in Bruges in 1529.

Death and the Miser, reverse of the wings of a triptych

Donor with St Nicholas and
Donor's Wife with St Godeliva first quarter 16th century
Jan Provoost *c.* 1465–1529
Panels, 120.5 x 78.5 cm (left wing) and
120 x 79 cm
Wings of a triptych
(reverse) *Death and the Miser*

These panels were originally the wings of a triptych, the centre panel of which is now lost. The donors appeared on the inside. When the triptych was closed, it showed the image of *Death and the Miser*. At some stage, the panels were sawn apart to separate the fronts and backs, which are now displayed separately.

The donors kneel in prayer in a small, enclosed garden. The view in the background includes scenes from the legends of their patron saints Nicholas and Godeliva. When the city of Myra faced starvation, Bishop Nicholas had a shipload of grain that was destined for Alexandria distributed among the people. When the vessel put into Alexandria for unloading, the cargo was found to have been miraculously replenished. Provoost places the episode in Antwerp: the tower we see being constructed is that of the Cathedral of Our Lady, while the dock with its crane was a famous Antwerp landmark (the 'Kraanhoofd'). The portico behind the donor and his patron saint originally had a different form – the initial design can be made out where the paint has worn. The woman in the right-hand panel is accompanied by her patron saint, Godeliva of Gistel. We see in the background how this holy benefactress met her death. The red carnations in the earthenware pot are a symbol of God's love and hence a reference to the name 'Godeliva'.

The meaning of the scene on the rear of the panels is not clear (p. 46). The supposed miser is a money-changer involved in some kind of transaction with Death, probably involving a church service for a deceased person. The onlooker in the doorway is almost certainly a self-portrait of Jan Provoost.

This 'Judgement' scene was painted for the Council Chamber of Bruges Town Hall. It was intended to remind the city magistrates of their duty to mete out justice impartially.

The iconographical programme is fairly original. Jesus displays the wound in his side and Mary bares her breast to signify their mercy. They are to intercede with God the Father on behalf of the faithful. A ray of golden light shoots from Christ's eye towards the blessed souls entering paradise. At the same time, he holds the traditional sword of judgement in his left hand. In the distance, we see the selected ones being transported to heaven by water, while in the lower right corner a hellish procession in the manner of Hieronymus Bosch enters the eternal flames. Almost all the damned souls are clergy, possibly personifying the Seven Deadly Sins. In 1550, 25 years after the painting was completed, the Council had the hell scene overpainted in accordance with a decree from Emperor Charles V that forbade disreputable images of churchmen and women. The overpainting was not removed until 1965, some four hundred years later.

The most striking part of this painting is its gold and brown frame. It is decorated with grotesques – an ornamental form derived from ancient Rome and the Italian Renaissance, consisting of vines and figural motifs. The people, animals, fruit and architectural elements combine to create a frivolous and luxuriant impression. The artist uses the device here to create the illusion of depth and sculptural volume.

Mary poses with her baby for St Luke, who is painting her portrait. The scene is set in an artist's studio, in which an apprentice can be seen in a side-room grinding pigment for the paint. The subtly coloured main theme only occupies a small part of the overall surface of the canvas, giving the effect of a precious medallion. The fabulous architectural setting does, however, redirects our attention to the central theme.

Lancelot Blondeel was a master at this type of ornamentation. His monogram – LAB with a little trowel – appears at the lower edge of the central scene, alongside the year 1545.

Lancelot Blondeel was an important figure in the first generation of Bruges Renaissance artists. He was very much the *uomo universale* – the modern, versatile and individualistic artist along Italian lines. His work includes paintings, drawings, maps and architectural and sculptural designs.

Because of their pronounced attention to ornamentation and decorative settings, the first painters to introduce Renaissance elements into the Flemish pictorial tradition came to be known as the 'Flemish Mannerists'

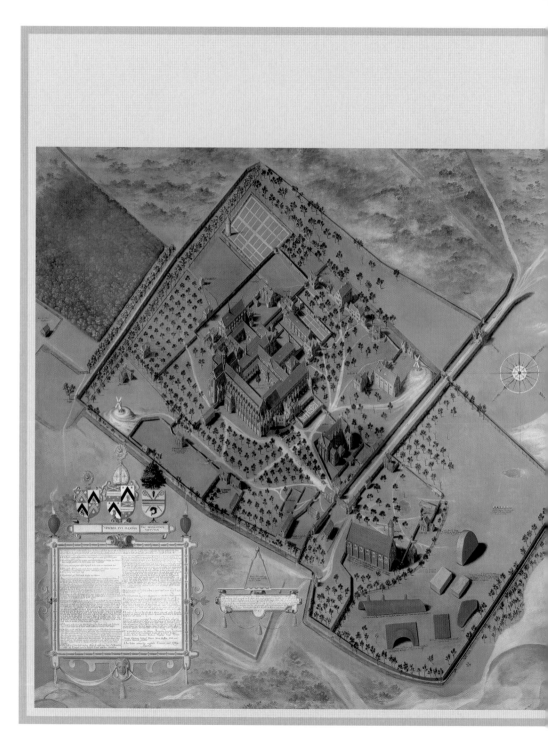

52

Pieter Pourbus enrolled in the Bruges painters' corporation in 1543, at the age of twenty. He came from the Northern Netherlands – probably Gouda – but had settled at a young age in Bruges, which still offered plenty of opportunities for artists. He married Lancelot Blondeel's daughter. Like his father-in-law, with whom he collaborated from time to time, Pourbus proved to be a versatile artistic personality. In addition to working as a draughtsman, cartographer, surveyor and engineer, he was the most important painter in Bruges in the second half of the 16th century. In 1549, the City Council commissioned him to design the festive decorations to mark the Joyful Entry of Crown Prince Philip of Spain (later Philip II) and his father, Emperor Charles V.

Pourbus is often referred to as the last Flemish Primitive, yet paintings like his *Last Judgement* clearly show that he was well aware of the latest developments of art from the very beginning of his career. His portraits are notable for their sober and sharp observation, and the skill with which he used pose, costume, expression and attributes like coats of arms to convey an individual's social status. The *Portraits of Jan van Eyewerve and Jacquemyne Buuck* illustrate his refined and restrained yet individualised portrait style.

In 1552, Pourbus bought a house in which he set up his studio. Carel van Mander praised it in his famous *Schilderboeck*: 'I never saw a better-equipped painter's workshop than his.' The artist's pupils included his son, Frans Pourbus the Elder, his grandson Frans Pourbus the Younger (see p. 60) and Antoon Claeissens (see p. 58).

Pieter Pourbus died in January 1584. He may have fallen victim to the plague that struck Bruges in that year.

Plan of Ter Duinen Abbey in Koksijde, 1580, canvas, 214.5 x 215 cm, painted 'model' of the powerful 'Abbey of the Dunes', which was destroyed by the Calvinists in 1578. The plan was to serve as an example in the event of the abbey's reconstruction

The Last Judgement 1551

Pieter Pourbus 1523/24–1584
Panel, 228.5 x 181 cm
Originally in the Palace of the Franc
of Bruges

Christ appears in the clouds, his arms outspread, separating the good from the wicked for all eternity. The lily and the sword held by the two small angels at the very top are symbols of salvation and damnation. As you will have noticed, there are several earlier images of the Last Judgement in the Groeninge Museum (pp. 38 and 50), so this painting requires little explanation. The dead rise from their graves, with the blessed souls making their way towards heaven, while the damned are herded into hell.

Pieter Pourbus incorporates a number of innovations in his presentation of the Last Day. He turns the entire episode into a single dramatic ensemble, with few details to suggest the social rank of the figures and without anecdotal elements like the gates of heaven or the burning mouth of hell. Together, these factors make the composition all the more imposing. The naked figures with their powerful, muscular bodies and sculptural volume are typically Renaissance. They move under their own power. The advances made in the representation of the human body become clear if this painting is compared with Jan Provoost's painting of the same subject.

Pourbus' main source of inspiration was Michelangelo's Last Judgement in the Sistine Chapel in the Vatican, completed ten years earlier. The fact that several figures and groups from that fresco are included here in reverse makes it almost certain that Pourbus based his painting on engravings (when a work of art is copied onto a copper plate, the resultant print is a mirror image of the original).

Michelangelo was not Pourbus' only source. He also borrowed figures from Jan Provoost, including, among the damned, the desperate woman with her fingers in her hair and, among the blessed, the woman who stands up with her hands clasped together. Pourbus was certainly familiar with Provoost's work, having been the artist ordered to overpaint the damned souls in his predecessor's panel in 1550!

Like Jan Provoost's Last Judgement, this version was destined for a Council Chamber. It hung in the Palace of the 'Brugse Vrije' or Franc of Bruges on the Burg in Bruges. The Franc of Bruges was a castellany in the County of Flanders. It consisted of the region between the Zwin estuary, the North Sea, the river IJzer and a line linking Diksmuide and Eeklo – an area taking in several towns.

If you view the picture from the side with the light falling at an angle, you can make out the different types of paint – some smoother, others coarser. The most striking colour is the blue, like the dress of the Virgin in heaven, on the left, and the drapery of the semi-nude figure to the right of Christ. To paint these zones, the artist used the pigment azurite. The resultant paint was grainy and difficult to use. It was normally applied on top of a darker layer in order to achieve a better colour effect, which means that these areas are a little thicker and more prone to wear. In Mary's cloak, either the azurite paint or the black layer beneath it has blistered.

All kinds of problem can arise as a painting ages. Sometimes the colours degenerate or fade, reveal-

ing the underdrawing. That phenomenon has occurred here in spectacular fashion: changes to the composition, hatching for the shadow zones and the outlines of figures have all now become visible. The demon in the lower right corner, for instance, originally sank his terrible claw into the thigh of one of the damned.

Portraits of Jan van Eyewerve and Jacquemyne Buuck 1551
Pieter Pourbus 1523/24–1584
Panels, 97.7 x 71.4 cm (left panel)
and 97.5 x 71.2 cm

The couple portrayed in these panels has been identified from the coats of arms as Jan van Eyewerve and his wife Jacquemyne Buuck. They were married in 1551 or 1552, which makes this painting a wedding portrait. The dog by Jacquemyne's side is a symbol of fidelity. Portraits like this were intended for the sitting-room, where they would be viewed from close quarters. Consequently, they were painted with particular care.

Husband and wife are located in the same room on either side of a window looking out onto Bruges' Kraanplaats and Vlamingbrug. The room appears to be located on the first floor of a house, possibly the couple's current or future home, on Vlamingstraat. The background scenes are attractively rendered.

Pieter Pourbus was a brilliant portraitist. The two figures are no doubt excellent likenesses, though without being too realistic. They are characterised with great refinement: the woman with her pale skin and elegant pose and the man with his powerful, frontal stance. The half-length view gives them a confident and somewhat monumental feel. Numerous details attest to their membership of the Bruges elite. The portraits lack spontaneity, but this will not have been a

AN DÑI·1551· ÆTATIS SVE· 19

OPVS PETRI
POVRBVS:

requirement – the couple will have been concerned about appearing distinguished. Likewise, strongly individualised features and psychological depth were not demanded and may even have been found undesirable. The main purpose of the painting is to convey the couple's social status.

Sitting-room portraits can be disconcerting if the subjects' gaze is fixed too firmly on the viewer. For that reason, Pourbus has his sitters looking discreetly and vaguely into the middle distance.

A comparison between these matching portraits and Jan van Eyck's painting of his wife Margareta (p. 15) or Adriaan Isenbrant's portrait of Paulus de Nigro (p. 40) reveals differences in style and mood that tell us something about social and artistic development in Bruges at that time.

Civil Servants' Banquet 1574

Antoon Claeissens c. 1536–1613
Panel, 130 x 155 cm
Originally in Bruges Town Hall

A whole range of factors can combine to change the appearance of the colours in a painting. In this case, the drapery in the background was originally cobalt blue. The smalt-based paint has, however, faded entirely. The pale greyish-green in the costumes is also the result of 'smalt failure'. Smalt consists of finely ground blue glass, with cobalt as its colouring agent. It was the cheapest blue pigment in Pourbus' day, but if it was ground too finely or mixed with oil, it tended to fade over time

Ten men in oriental costume sit around the table. Two hefty men in pseudo-Roman cuirass carry large wine-jugs. In the background, five women sit in a loggia at which a messenger has just arrived. Two excited-looking men hurry in from the right. The overall scene depicts a story from the Old Testament Book of Esther. King Ahasuerus of Persia and his lovely wife Vashti organised a great banquet – the king for the men and the queen for the women. When Vashti refused to come to the drunken king, he renounced her.

It is unclear why Bruges' civil servants chose to have themselves painted in the context of the Ahasuerus story. Two members of the company are named: on the base of a pillar on the far left we make out the name of Jan de Schietere; while that of Filips van Belle appears in the border of the headdress worn by the man in the richly decorated chair.

The antique costumes and stiff poses, the elegant still life on the table and the mishmash of Renaissance elements lend the painting a very theatrical yet naïve and charming air.

Antoon Claeissens belonged to a prominent family of Bruges artists. He learned his craft in his father's workshop, before entering that of Pieter Pourbus to complete his training. He was appointed municipal painter and completed a variety of commissions for the City Council, including this panel. The work hung originally in Bruges Town Hall. The precise occasion of its commission is unknown.

The man in this surprisingly realistic portrait has traditionally been identified as a physician, although the painting itself offers no evidence to this effect. His costume and expression certainly suggest that he is a scholar of some kind. His appearance corresponds with the typical Flemish humanist portrait, a popular type in Northern Renaissance painting.

The artist, Adriaan Key, worked in Antwerp. His work is characterised by its sober and photographic technique.

A strip approximately two centimetres wide has been added to all four sides of the panel. This operation, the results of which can be clearly seen, was probably undertaken to make the painting match another, slightly larger portrait.

The Latin inscription in the upper left corner identifies the subject of the portrait as 'Petrus Ricardus, professor at the University of Louvain and physician to His Majesty'. His coat of arms appears in the opposite corner, together with his motto *'Nil temere'* ('nothing rashly'). Petrus Ricardus (or Pieter Ryckaert) was municipal physician in Ghent and the personal physician to the archdukes Albert and Isabella, the governors of the Low Countries. His position is further emphasised by the books by Galen and Hippocrates on the table on the left.

The portrait style of Frans Pourbus the Younger was plainly influenced by that of Adriaan Key (p. 59). His portrait of Petrus Ricardus is executed in the same analytical and realistic manner as Key's *Portrait of a Man*. Frans Pourbus the Younger was born in Antwerp, where he most likely began his training as a child under his grandfather, Pieter Pourbus the Elder. He may then have entered the workshop of Adriaan Key. He later travelled to Mantua, where he became court painter to Vincenzo Gonzaga. Pourbus subsequently worked for Marie de' Medici and Louis XIII in Paris. He was one of the most successful court painters of his day.

St Martin c. 1656

Jacob van Oost the Elder 1601–1671
Canvas, 301 x 181 cm
Originally in the Convent of St Trudo,
Bruges

One cold winter's day, a Roman officer called Martin was riding up to the city gates of Amiens when he saw a half-naked beggar sitting on the ground. Martin had no money to give as alms, so he drew his sword, cut his cloak in two and gave half of it to the beggar.

This monumental depiction of the kindly saint derives from a famous composition that Anthony van Dyck painted around 1620. It is also influenced by the art of Italy, where Jacob van Oost spent a number of years. This is apparent in the Caravaggesque treatment of the light, with its characteristically heavy chiaroscuro contrast, which reinforces the dramatic and theatrical mood of the scene. For the rest, Van Oost was a sedate, 'early Baroque' painter, especially if we compare him to his slightly older contemporaries in Antwerp – the exuberant Rubens and Jordaens and the aristocratic Van Dyck.

In 1656–57, Van Oost presented this and a number of other paintings to the Augustinian Convent of St Trudo, which his daughter Maria had recently entered.

Jacob van Oost the Elder was the most important figure in 17th-century Bruges painting, producing numerous altarpieces for churches and abbeys in Bruges, and non-religious works like allegories and genre pieces. He was the favourite portraitist of the Bruges bourgeoisie. As a young man, he spent a number of years in Italy and the influence of Italian early Baroque painting was to remain a tangible part of his style throughout his career.

The wealthy burgher who is the
focal point of this painting proudly
draws our attention to his 'posses-
sions'. The estate that stretches into
the distance belongs to him, as do
the happy woman at his side and the
children around him. The children's
maid and the gardener are in his service, and the terrace on which he
stands indicates the grandeur of his
house. The painter has adopted a
very low viewpoint, which lends
the company – and the father in particular – a very imposing air. In
other words, there is a great deal
going on beneath the surface of
what is seemingly a naïve and idyllic
scene. On the one hand, the portrait
glorifies a family life based on love
and fertility, while on the other, it
affirms the family's social status.
Wealthy bourgeois in the 17th century yearned to join the ranks of the
aristocracy – an ambition that could
be fulfilled by purchasing an estate
with an associated title of nobility.
The man in this portrait clearly has
aristocratic aspirations.

The family portrait shows a
Bruges family, with the city itself ris-
ing up on the skyline. The ages of the
family members are incorporated in
the painting in the manner of a puz-
zle. The man is 46, as we see from the
heel of his shoe. His wife's age (26)
appears on her fan and that of the boy
next to her (3) on his hat. The girl
sitting on the cushion is 15 (age on
her basket), the youth is 17 (boot)
and the baby in the maid's arms is
one year old (hands). Their respective ages indicate that these are chil-

dren of two separate marriages. The
woman in the painting is probably
the mother of the two little ones.

The artist's signature and date
appear on the balustrade, between
the man's calves. With its fresh,
country atmosphere, sparkling sunlight and underlying symbolism,
this family portrait is Jacob van
Oost the Elder's masterpiece.

The still life as an autonomous genre arose in Western European painting towards the end of the 16th century. Elements of still life had been featured before that, but never as a theme in their own right. They were used instead as a part of the overall composition or to embellish the setting. An attractive example can be seen in Antoon Claeissens' 1574 *Civil Servants' Banquet* (see p. 58).

Several sub-genres quickly arose within the still-life theme: floral pieces, still lifes with game, fruit or fish and tabletop still lifes like 'breakfasts' and 'banquets'. Many painters concentrated on a single strand, in which they attained a very high level. Apart from a few fruit and flower still lifes, all Alexander Adriaenssen's surviving paintings feature fish. Still lifes with fish were not the easiest speciality, given the specific appearance of their subject, but Adriaenssen was extremely adept at capturing the silvery skin, the scales and the pearly flesh. Characteristic features of his style include the diagonal, asymmetrical structure and the sober, almost monochrome palette.

In this case, the description 'still life' is somewhat deceptive, as the prowling cat is about to turn the composition upside-down.

The children seem to be taking a breather in the portico, which looks out over the garden where they have just been playing. The oldest child, a girl, stands up straight. Each of the three younger ones has a prop – a little basket of apples, a dog on a lead or a whip for spinning a top. These attributes may have a deeper significance. The apples, for instance, suggest a family blessed with children, the dog is a symbol of fidelity, and the whip alludes to raising children with a firm hand.

Nicolaas Maes was born in Dordrecht and was apprenticed to Rembrandt in Amsterdam around 1650. His early works show the influence of his teacher's chiaroscuro style. He also spent some time in Antwerp before settling permanently in Amsterdam. In addition to his subtle and fashionable portraits, Maes also painted genre pieces on the theme of domestic life.

Achilles and the Daughters of Lycomedes mid-17th century
Erasmus Quellinus 1607–1678
Canvas, 220 x 240 cm

Knowing that her son Achilles would be killed in the Trojan War, Thetis advised him to go into hiding. He dressed in women's clothing and entered the court of King Lycomedes. The Greek commanders, Odysseus and Diomedes, realised that they could not win the war without their bravest warrior and so consulted a soothsayer who told them where Achilles was hiding. To trick him into revealing himself, they visited King Lycomedes and offered gifts, including weapons, to his daughters and the disguised hero. Achilles automatically reached for the helmet and sword, giving himself away. His sense of duty now took over and he joined his comrades as they set off to do battle.

The story is recounted here with great flourish. The painter even manages to signal the romance between Achilles and Deidameia, one of Lycomedes' daughters. The girl sits next to her beloved with an expression that speaks volumes.

Erasmus Quellinus belonged to an Antwerp family of sculptors, painters, etchers and woodcarvers. He was a pupil and assistant of Rubens, whom he succeeded as Antwerp's city painter. In that capacity, he painted many religious and secular history paintings. He was one of the most productive artists in Rubens' circle.

Still Life with Fowl second half 17th century
Frans Cuyck van Myerop c. 1640–1689
Canvas, 120 x 93 cm

As time passed, more and more attention was paid to the realistic representation of nature, people and things – a traditional concern of Flemish painters ever since Jan van Eyck. This development was accompanied in the 16th and 17th centuries with a burgeoning interest on the part of artists and patrons for non-religious subjects – mythological scenes, portraits, genre paintings and still lifes. In the era before photography, one of the painter's tasks was to evoke reality convincingly in two dimensions. Yet this realism was never entirely innocent – it was always placed in the service of an underlying idea. It would be wrong to think, for instance, that the Bruges artist Frans Cuyck van Myerop painted these three birds (a bittern, a small wader and a songbird) in such a precise *trompe-l'œil* manner purely to show off his virtuosity. This is, in fact, a 'vanitas' painting – a symbol of the transience and vanity of earthly existence. The genre was very popular in the 17th century. The dead birds recall the fleeting nature of life, while the illusionistic image symbolises the deceptive appearance of the visible world.

The expansive, cloud-filled sky, the tall ships with their billowing sails and fluttering pennants, the small, busy figures in the foreground and the hazy townscape in the distance combine to evoke that special harbour atmosphere of distant voyages and exotic destinations.

This Baroque harbour view was probably painted to mark the opening of the new Town Docks or 'Handelskom' in Bruges, in 1665, which means the year '1653' that appears bottom centre is incorrect. It was probably added in the 19th century because of an erroneous interpretation of an inscription in the painting itself. The festively rigged ship that has just fired its cannon is identified on its stern as the *Viva Vlanderen*, built in 1653.

The painter Hendrik van Minderhout was born in Rotterdam but settled in Bruges at the age of twenty. He moved to Antwerp twenty years later and remained there until his death. He specialised in magnificent harbour views, often with a Mediterranean or exotic flavour.

Flower Still Life c. 1700

Gaspar-Peter Verbruggen
the Younger 1664–1730
Canvas, 98 x 71.5 cm
Original limewood frame
by Laurent van der Meulen 1645–1719

From the late 16th century onwards, particularly in Antwerp, a high degree of specialisation developed in individual sub-genres. In some cases, this was passed on from father to son – after all, it had long been customary for painters to train their own offspring in their workshops. An early and famous example of such a painters' dynasty was provided by the Bruegel family. The style and themes of Pieter Bruegel the Elder were faithfully adopted by his eldest son, also called Pieter. There are countless examples of similar traditions. The Antwerp artist Gaspar-Peter Verbruggen the Younger followed in the footsteps of his father, the floral painter Gaspar-Peter Verbruggen the Elder. The Groeninge Museum has several of the son's works. They consist for the most part of lively flower arrangements in antique-style vases or sculptural settings. Their late-Baroque luxuriance and atmospheric lighting give them an especially attractive appearance. The charm of this flower still life is further enhanced by its marvellous limewood frame.

The Garden of the Willaeys-Vleys Family at Groeninge, Bruges 1759
Bruges master 18th century
Canvas, 178.5 x 92.5 cm

This view of Bruges is a 'topographical landscape', in which the painter offers a precise image of a section of the city environment. The work was probably commissioned by the owner of the depicted plot. In the second half of the 18th century, large compositions like this were mounted in the panelling of drawing-rooms, dining-rooms and studies.

The city is seen from the southeast with the Groeninge district appearing in the foreground. Silhouetted against the skyline are, from left to right, the tower of Our Lady's Church, the Gruuthuse mansion, the squat tower of Holy Saviour's, what is now the administrative building of the Groeninge Museum (with the black and red roof), the Belfry and the imposing Eekhout Abbey. The current museum was later built on the site of the orchard on the right.

Before the topographical landscape became a genre in its own right, it began to crop up in the background of portraits and religious images in the form of detailed townscapes. Several examples are to be found in the museum's collection.

The date or the artist's signature are often incorporated in an original way in Old Master paintings. In this case, the painting is dated on the wheelbarrow shown lower centre.

The setting sun breaks through the clouds, possibly heralding the end of the storm. Meanwhile, ship-wrecked sailors are being pulled out of the water. Debris from a capsized three-master is washed up on the shore. A steep cliff topped with a fortress looms ominously out of the darkness. The human tragedy occasioned by the elemental force of nature makes the sublime beauty of the angry sea and the dramatic, cloudy sky lit by the evening sun even more impressive.

The French landscape painter Claude Joseph Vernet was a master of the storm-at-sea genre. Having worked in Rome for many years, he moved to Paris in 1753, where he embarked on a series of views of French harbours. He subsequently concentrated on storms at sea – a speciality for which he gained an outstanding reputation, but which gradually began to slip into routine. His style is a synthesis of 17th-century Italian and French landscape painting.

In this example, he creates a magnificent spectacle in an almost Romantic manner that far transcends the picturesque.

This unbelievable panorama containing hundreds of figures shows
the digging of the canal between
Bruges and Ghent. Not only is the
painting an artistic *tour de force*, it is
also an important historical docu-
ment. The excavation of the Ghent
Canal began in 1751 at the order of
the Austrian authorities. Such a
large-scale project required the creation of a temporary construction
site. Tents were provided as accom-
modation for around three and a
half thousand labourers.

The artist began by making a
number of sketches from life, which
he combined in this overwhelming panorama. The most fascinating
aspects of the painting are its atmospheric colours and the brilliance
with which the figures are drawn.
The countless little personages are
rendered in a lively rococo style.

Garemijn's masterpiece (originally a single canvas that was later
split into two) belonged for many
years to the collection of Count Karl
von Cobenzl, plenipotentiary in the
Southern Netherlands of the
Empress Maria-Theresa.

The stirring and frequently bombastic art of the Baroque gradually gave way in the early 18th century to a new style – the playful and charming rococo. Artists no longer sought to overwhelm or move, but simply to charm their viewers with light-hearted themes. In France, Jean Antoine Watteau, François Boucher and Jean Honoré Fragonard created a soft-coloured dreamworld peopled by gallant companies in shady gardens, shepherds and shepherdesses in idyllic settings and sweet interiors. Although this art may appear superficial, it often exudes a poetic and even melancholy atmosphere, certainly in Watteau.

Flemish rococo artists were unable to match the poetry or aristocratic elegance of the French masters, but they still managed to produce a fresh, bourgeois drawing-room style.

Jan Antoon Garemijn was the most talented practitioner of this rather provincial strand of rococo art. Born in Bruges, he spent his entire life in the city. Garemijn painted landscapes, portraits, bourgeois interiors and genre scenes, including *The Pandreitje in Bruges*.

The Pandreitje – a square in Bruges – was home to the vegetable market. Countrywomen have laid out their vegetables in the foreground. In the background, meanwhile, we see the butchers selling their wares in the portico of the former jail. A street entertainer sings songs and cracks jokes for the benefit of marketgoers. He seems to be selling *mannekensbladen* – a kind of

18th-century Flemish illustrated paper containing sensational stories. The picture behind him bears the incomplete inscription 'WVN-DERLYCKL VAN – 1778' (Wonderful stories [?] of 1778).

Garemijn devoted plenty of attention to anecdote and picturesque detail in his canvases. Market scenes offered an idealised image of the common people, without the symbolism and moralising undertone that earlier artists had inserted into similar themes and certainly without any intended social criticism.

Portrait of the Villers Family 1790   Jan Bernard Duvivier 1762–1837
Canvas, 112 x 145 cm

This lovely family portrait was painted in 1790 by a Bruges artist who lived and worked in Paris in the turbulent years after the French Revolution.

The subjects have traditionally been identified as a family called Villers, which some art historians have identified as that of Marc-Etienne de Villiers du Terrage. This *gentilhomme* was a senior civil servant during the ancien régime. He naturally fell from grace in 1789, the year of the Revolution, and, like so many other aristocrats, was sentenced to death. He escaped the guillotine, however, because an agent of the Social Welfare Committee had him imprisoned at a different jail to the other condemned nobles. His son René-Edouard was also arrested and experienced the Terror at first hand. Following his release, he went on to study engineering. He took part in Napoleon Bonaparte's famous expedition to Egypt between 1798 and 1801 as a member of the 'Commission des Sciences et Arts d'Egypte'. The group portrait also includes the mother, who had died in 1788, and two daughters – assuming, of course, that this really is the Villiers du Terrage family, which is far from certain. Whoever they are, the family is in every way representative of an entire social class in revolutionary France, the character of which is perfectly conveyed in this portrait.

The central theme of the painting is that of fidelity. That virtue is represented in the oval grisaille by a female figure, who strokes a dog while holding the laurel wreath of victory in her other hand. Fidelity was seen as the foundation stone of domestic happiness, while for the nobleman it was also important in the sense of loyalty to king and country. This dual significance lends a tragic undertone to this apparently happy scene. Current events – rioting against the king and aristocracy and the abolition of noble and ecclesiastical privileges in 1790 – were, after all, ominous signs. The deathknell was being rung for the refined lifestyle of the aristocracy.

The painter undoubtedly had these circumstances in mind when he captured the family's Louis XVI drawing-room on canvas. He records their cosy interior, their silk and lace costumes and their pastimes with extraordinary precision, as wishing to preserve the memory of it all. The musical instruments, library, globe and works of art testify to the cultivated family's interests. The way the eyes are rendered is also intriguing – they bulge slightly and have a penetrating gleam. The painting's technical perfection ensures that it has lost none of its intrigue.

At some stage, Duvivier made a number of adjustments to the background. The window with its awning and the urn with the two caryatids are both additions. The original configuration has gradually shown through over time, revealing traces of a wall decoration with round, decorative frames that may have been the setting for a painting.

Jan Bernard Duvivier was born in Bruges and received his initial painter's training at the city's Academy of Fine Arts. He then continued his studies in Paris and later in Italy. He arrived in Rome in 1790, but also spent time in Florence and Venice before returning to Paris in 1796. Duvivier adhered entirely to the classical style of Jacques Louis David. He was appointed professor at the Ecole Normale and spent the rest of his life in Paris.

If you think back for a moment to the paintings of the rococo artist Jan Antoon Garemijn and then examine this *Invention of the Art of Drawing*, you will appreciate how much western society had developed in the space of a few decades. Joy and elegance had given way to seriousness and classical rigour. The new neoclassical art found a receptive home in Bruges at the Academy, which enjoyed great prestige by the end of the 18th century.

A variety of Bruges artists won international fame and spread out to Rome and Paris – the capitals of Neoclassicism.

Neoclassicism was an academic school of art, which was taught in academies using examples from antiquity. The style is sober, cool, rational and static, with drawing – the purity of the line – taking precedence over colour. Favourite genres at the time were history paintings, with themes from classical antiquity, and the portrait.

The drawing-room window looks onto the Rotonde de Reuilly, a building near Paris. The bare tree suggests that it was wintertime. The family portrait must, therefore, have been done in the French capital in early 1790, before Duvivier left for Rome (April). He was to spend several years there, well out of reach of the French Revolution.

The way in which the French tricolour is incorporated in the painting – in the feathers on the hat, the strings of the harp and elsewhere – is a significant, if contrived expression of patriotic sentiment

Having trained at the Academy in his native Bruges, **Joseph Benoît Suvée** moved to Paris where he was appointed teacher at the Académie Gratuite de Dessin in 1767. He was awarded the much-coveted Prix de Rome in 1771, beating Jacques Louis David, who was to become the figurehead of Neoclassicism. He spent the period 1772–78 in Rome. In 1780, he was appointed Painter to the King in Paris and became a member of the

Joseph Benoît Suvée 1743–1807
Canvas, 267 x 131.5 cm

In this painting, Joseph Suvée recounts the classical myth of the invention of the art of drawing. Dibutades, daughter of the potter Butades, traced her beloved's shadow on the wall of her father's workshop so that she could see him even when he was absent. The painting features all the characteristics of neoclassical art, from the choice of theme to the sober composition, cool palette and sharp outlines. The underlying idea draws on Platonic philosophy, which viewed art as the shade of reality.

Académie Royale de Peinture et de Sculpture. He was appointed director of the Académie de France in Rome in 1792. David, who was still smarting from the Prix de Rome incident, had the latter appointment overturned and even managed to get Suvée thrown into prison! Suvée was rehabilitated, however, and did eventually become director of the Académie de France in 1801. His work consists primarily of history scenes and portraits.

The serious-looking girl who poses so naturally in this portrait was the painter's niece. Franciscus van der Donckt came from Aalst and received his initial training at the Academy in Bruges, where his teachers included Garemijn. Like so many of his Bruges colleagues, he spent a good deal of time in Paris, before eventually being appointed director of the Bruges Academy. He specialised in portraiture.

The varied and realistic rendering of materials and attention to detail have always been characteristic of Flemish art. The refined painting technique is striking even in the work of a less renowned master like Van der Donckt. See, for example, how he handles the different fabrics and the hair of the dog, and the way he contrasts their lively textures with the dark background and wooden floor.

In 1818, Sylvie de la Rue married the Bruges neoclassical artist Joseph Odevaere (1775–1830), who went on to become court painter to King William I of the Netherlands. Several of Odevaere's paintings can be seen in the Groeninge Museum.

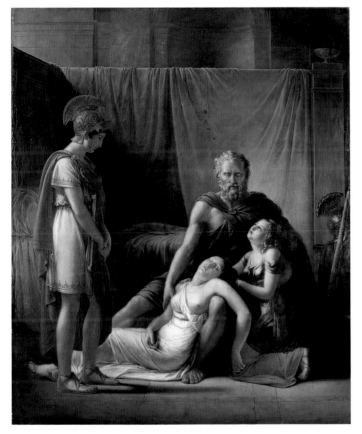

Portrait of Marie-Joséphine Lafont-Porcher, c. 1830, canvas, 100 x 81 cm. The subject was an opera singer in Paris and was married to the famous French violinist Charles Lafont. Her literary salon received the elite of the artistic world, including Alexandre Dumas

History painting – *le grand genre* – enjoyed great prestige in the 17th, 18th and 19th centuries. Indeed it represented the highest an artist could achieve. The grand style often seems bombastic and theatrical to the modern viewer – an impression that is further heightened by the customary large scale of the paintings. Paintings like this were not, of course, destined for the parlour.

They hung instead in public buildings, where they reminded passersby of the great virtues and social values that had been passed down since classical civilisation.

François Kinsoen composed *The Death of Belisarius' Wife* entirely in accordance with the strict and rational rules of neoclassical art. The scene is based on an episode in the successful novel

Bélisaire (1767), which told the tragic story of a Roman general from the reign of Emperor Justinian. The loyal Belisarius was wrongly accused of treason and Justinian ordered that he be blinded. When the hero returned home in disgrace, his wife Antonina was so stricken that she died.

This is, in fact, the only history painting by François Kinsoen of Bruges, who earned great fame in Paris and elsewhere as a portraitist. His elegant female portraits are among the finest works produced by the Bruges neoclassical school.

Landscape with Cows near Oudenaarde 1843
Jean-Baptiste Daveloose 1807–1886
Canvas, 61 x 81.5 cm

Landscape painting developed and renewed itself in the 19th century. Artists left their academies and studios and began to work in the open air. Direct observation sparked a revolution in the genre. Not only did the vision of nature now change, but also the way in which nature was represented. The image became livelier and more realistic, and the brushwork more spontaneous. Having abandoned the confinement of the studio, artists became fascinated with the never-ending shifts of light and atmosphere as the day advanced and the weather and seasons changed. The museum contains a variety of views of nature, the sea and the town that combine to illustrate the diversity of this fascinating genre.

This expansive view of the Scheldt valley largely remains a classically composed 'studio landscape' in the spirit of the 17th-century Dutch and Flemish landscape painters. The pattern of the brown foreground, green central zone and hazy blue horizon dates back to the panoramic 'world landscape' of the 16th century. A similar breakdown into three zones can be seen, for instance, in Pieter Pourbus' *Last Judgement* (p. 55) and, even earlier than that, in the triptych by the Master of the Holy Blood (p. 41). Yet Daveloose's landscape also offers something new – a Romantic feeling for nature – in its treatment of the light and mood.

A young woman puts the finishing touches to her appearance in a room with a 17th-century feel. No doubt she is about to visit an acquaintance or to receive visitors herself. Florent Willems successfully evokes the elegant lifestyle of the mid-19th-century bourgeoisie, placing it in a setting that recalls the style of the 17th-century Dutch masters, of whom he was a great admirer.

Literature and the visual arts began to react around 1800 to the rigour and rationality of Neoclassicism. Romanticism came to dominate the first half of the 19th century. One of the movement's characteristics was its interest in the past – especially the Middle Ages and the 16th and 17th centuries. One thing this overenthusiastic school lacked, however, was realism. As time passed, many artists thus began to focus on a more faithful representation of reality. With his penchant for sentimentality and the art of the Dutch Golden Age, Florent Willems and his attractive interiors lined up firmly with Romantic art. By contrast, his urge to represent objects, fabrics and people as precisely and attractively as possible, with no motive other than art for art's sake, is typical of Realism.

As a young artist, **Florent Willems** moved from his native Liège to Paris. He achieved a great deal of success there with his portraits, genre pieces and interiors, most of which he gave a 16th- or 17th-century feel. Also striking is the skilful way in which he represented expensive fabrics like brocade and silk.

It is late afternoon in the high mountains and the sun has already begun to cast a reddish light onto the rocks. The overwhelming beauty of the mountains appealed to Romantic artists. In such a grandiose space, they saw the reflection of the soul with its lofty emotions. The Belgian artist François-Xavier Roffiaen painted many sublime Alpine landscapes, which he rendered with photographic realism and a smooth painting technique. His work falls within the transition between the academic and the natural, realistic landscape.

The Brussels critic Camille Lemonnier summed up the evolution towards greater naturalism in 19th-century landscape painting in these words: 'The moist fragrance of the open air begins to register. One feels the breakthrough of an intimate perception of nature, a love of light and a new feeling for the dawn and the setting of the sun. The spirit is roused by the vibration of the leaves, the joy of the sunshine and the whispering of the wind. At the same time, the artist seeks the right tones with which to represent nature, the harmony of plains and treetops – the soft, deep blue of the sky.'

Hippolyte Boulenger was the most important Belgian exponent of the new landscape vision. Following the example of the Romantic realism of the French Barbizon School, he abandoned the academic, composed landscape in favour of the intense contact with nature he experienced by painting *'en plein air'*. He became the leading figure in the 'Tervuren School', so called because he lived for a while in Tervuren, near Brussels, where a group of *pleinairists* formed around him.

The Brussels artist Alphonse Asselbergs was a member of that group. He worked not only around Brussels, but in the Ardennes, the Kempen region and at Barbizon (France). Like Boulenger, he worked in a fluid pictorial style with natural, earth colours. His melancholic and Romantic character inspired him to paint wistful landscapes that combine emotion with the observation of nature.

In this early work, Emile Claus tackles his favourite theme – rural life on the banks of the river Lys near Astene, in the province of East Flanders. He spent his summers in the area, before settling there permanently in 1886. He continued throughout his life to paint sunny images of country people and nature, though his style evolved later, in the 1890s, in the direction of Impressionism.

He began his career painting genre pieces in the naturalistic and anecdotal style that was popular at the time throughout Europe. It may be described as a sort of 'bright' realism, in that the form and content are faithful to reality, but the 'dirty' earth and forest colours of his predecessors are now giving way to a brighter and lighter palette. The painting discussed here belongs to this early part of the painter's career.

Sunlight was crucial in Claus' work. The back-lighting of the two children is a charming procedure that he used on a number of occasions. As time passed, and especially in his later Impressionist or 'Luminist' canvases, the light that is already a vital presence in *The River Lys at Astene* became an all-embracing summer sunlight.

Portrait of Laurent in Blankenberge c. 1888
Henry van de Velde 1863–1957
Canvas, 44 × 34 cm

Artistic life in Belgium began to flourish in the final decades of the 19th century. Avant-garde art societies popped up, especially in Brussels, the members of which maintained close ties with their counterparts in Paris. One of the nuclei at which new ideas were developed and foreign innovations eagerly tracked was the association known as 'Les XX' ('les vingt' or 'the twenty'). Every year, the Salon of Les XX greeted the very latest trends in art. The 1887 Salon, for instance, saw the introduction of Neo-Impressionism to Belgium with the presentation of Georges Seurat's painting *Un dimanche après-midi à la Grande Jatte.* Many artists, including the young Henry van de Velde, were immediately won over by the new style. The key feature of Neo-Impressionism (also known as 'pointillism' and 'divisionism') is its use of unblended colours, which are applied to the canvas in adjacent dots according to the theory of complementary colours. Van de Velde threw himself into this time-consuming technique. In this *Portrait of Laurent in Blankenberge,* which was probably painted the following year, he chanced his arm at a modest and not entirely orthodox pointillist background. A year later, in the summer of 1889, he produced a series of Neo-Impressionist masterpieces. This portrait of his brother thus represents an important stage in his career. It is also one of the first pointillist experiments to be attempted in Belgium.

The Antwerp painter **Henry van de Velde** is viewed as one of the pioneers of Art Nouveau in Belgium. He worked as a painter, interior designer, teacher, writer and typographer. Having devoted himself to painting for ten years, he abandoned it in 1894 to concentrate exclusively on decorative art and architecture – fields in which he produced further pioneering work.

The Virgin Inspiring the Arts c. 1893

Edmond Van Hove 1851–1913
Canvas, 177 x 239 cm

The world we see here bathed in a bright, hazy light is not our own. This is a mystical world, evoked in a Renaissance setting and populated with figures reminiscent of Raphael. Symbolic images like this, rendered in an idealised and sentimental style, became a new trend in the late 19th century throughout Europe. They reflected the *fin de siècle* spirit, which displayed a marked interest in the past and a penchant for the mystical and esoteric. In a rapidly changing society, full of contrasts, artists sought a haven in Gothic, early Netherlandish and Italian Renaissance art, the spiritual depth of which they tried to imbue in their own work.

Edmond Van Hove was swept up by the international Symbolist movement. His enthusiasm was natural, because as a native of Bruges, he found himself close to the source of this new art. He trained at the Bruges Academy, the museum of which (the precursor of the Groeninge) contained panels by Van Eyck and Memling. As a young artist, he spent several years in Paris, where he studied under Alexandre Cabanel, a French academic painter who was best known for the overblown works he produced on behalf of the government. Van Hove earned a living by copying paintings in the Louvre, which brought him into even more intensive contact with the Old Masters and helped him to develop his flawless technique.

Van Hove initially concentrated on portraits, genre paintings and medieval figures and occupations, in a smooth and razor-sharp style borrowed from the Flemish Primitives. Despite his realistic and minutely detailed technique,

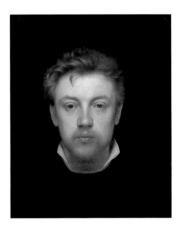

Self-portrait, 1879, canvas, 46 x 38 cm

his paintings have a strange air of unreality. The portraits, including his *Self-portrait*, are executed in a deep and dark palette comprising black and brown tones. In the 1890s, he also began to paint religious and allegorical works in a brighter and more colourful palette. He attached a great deal of importance to the frames of his canvases, as we see in *The Virgin Inspiring the Arts*.

Edmond Van Hove included a number of historical figures in the background. On the left-hand side, we see Dante talking to a monk (probably Thomas Aquinas) and Albrecht Dürer and Michelangelo. On the right, Hans Memling looks over the low wall, while behind him Erasmus talks to another humanist

A Venetian *palazzo* appears through the darkness, deep blue and velvety. The image is permeated with the artist's state of mind.

Venice fascinated William Degouve de Nuncques. In that place with its centuries-old palaces, reflecting in the sparkling water, he found the perfect setting for his melancholic and dark thoughts. It was not the picturesque Venice of *palazzi*, canal views, little bridges and gondeliers that attracted him, but the gloom of the city on the lagoon where invisible gondolas slip by silently in the darkness, where ghosts of the past haunt the secretive inner courtyards, and where the façade of a building, veiled in darkness, looms like the final witness of a sunken city. The Symbolist poet Emile Verhaeren called Degouve de Nuncques the 'discoverer of the soul of things'. The painter himself summed up the essence of his work as follows: 'To make a painting, all you have to do is to take colours, draw lines and fill in the rest with emotion.'

Works like this placed William Degouve de Nuncques in the idealist tendency within the Symbolist movement of the 1890s – 'idealist' in the sense that this brand of Symbolism was oriented towards the transcendental and invisible. This was an elitist art, practised by hypersensitive and introverted personalities, who rejected realism and the academic art of the salons with equal firmness. They wished to devote themselves purely to the secrets of the soul. Their paintings exude a decadent and bourgeois atmosphere, sometimes with a psychoanalytical undertone. Apart from Degouve de Nuncques, the key figures in Belgian idealist Symbolism included Fernand Khnopff and Jean Delville. All three worked primarily in Brussels in the final decades of the 19th and the early part of the 20th century. The Groeninge Museum has several important works by each of them.

William Degouve de Nuncques belonged to an old French aristocratic family with a long-standing interest in art. When he was three, he moved to Bruges with his parents. He devoted himself from a young age to the study of nature and to exploring his own imagination. As he grew up, he became bound up more and more with his own moods. He eventually became a self-taught painter, frequenting the circle of Symbolist painters and writers in Brussels and Paris. He spent a lot of time travelling around Europe, looking for the place that would best match his mental world. The most interesting phase in his career was the Symbolist period, which lasted from around 1892 to 1900. The works he produced in those years are pervaded with an enigmatic poetry – a silence full of yearning.

George Minne owes his reputation primarily to his early sculptures, which he produced before 1900. They embody the emotional world of the Symbolists – the kneeling, nude boy, mother and child in tragic lamentation and the Holy Women. These small, sober works radiate an imposing spiritual strength. With their simplified design and expressiveness, they can even be considered early manifestations of Expressionism.

Medieval art was an important source of inspiration for Minne. This small group of Holy Women in mourning dress seems to derive from a Gothic past. The figures recall the *pleurants* – small weeping figures – that decorated late-medieval mausolea.

Minne modelled his sculptures rather than carving them in stone or wood. Having fashioned his image in clay, he had a plastercast made, which was then used as the basis for a bronze, stone or wooden version.

It is sometimes claimed that a propensity towards mysticism is a characteristic of the Flemish, and by extension the Belgian national character. Coming face to face with Minne's art, you certainly cannot help feeling a sense of spirituality that has been passed down the ages.

As a student in Ghent **George Minne** began to frequent the circle of Symbolist poets, who were quick to admire the young artist's achievements. He spent the period 1895–99 in Brussels, where he joined the progressive artistic society Les XX. Minne also came into contact with modern art in Paris, Vienna and Berlin – the leading centres of Art Nouveau. In 1899, he settled in Sint-Martens-Latem – a village on the river Lys, near Ghent. He was a member of a small artist's colony there, which came to be known as the 'first group of Latem'. He later died at the village.

The French painter and draughts-man Henri Le Sidaner visited Bruges for the first time in July 1898. He immediately found what he had been looking for – a dreamy atmosphere capable of inspiring symbolically charged and atmospheric paintings. The city bewitched Le Sidaner. He painted a variety of works in that period, including *The Quay*, with its view of Bruges' Lange Rei. A sense of mystery is evoked by the twilight, the reflections in the water and the unreal houses. Unlike Degouve de Nuncques, however, Le Sidaner's reverie is not gloomy. Lamps are lit in several of the houses and the illuminated windows are reassuring. Emile Verhaeren once said that Le Sidaner could make you 'feel the silence'. 'You feel,' Verhaeren went on, 'as if you are looking through a window in the dead town, from which you are an unseen witness of the quiet and centuries-old death-struggle of bricks, trees and squares.'

Secret-Reflet 1902

Fernand Khnopff 1858–1921
Pastel and colour pencil on paper,
49.5 cm (diam.) and 27.8 x 49 cm

Bruges has an odd relationship with Symbolism. The Belgian writer Georges Rodenbach made the city world-famous with his novel *Bruges-la-morte* (1892). Bruges was saddled in that book with a gloomy image of silence, melancholy, reverie, loneliness, decline and death – qualities that it was rapidly taken to symbolise. The painter Fernand Khnopff, who designed the title-page for *Bruges-la-morte*, was also obsessed by the decadent beauty of the Venice of the North.

Khnopff spent part of his childhood in Bruges and remembered the city in later life, when he lived and worked in Brussels: 'I spent my youth in Bruges, which was a truly dead city at the time and still entirely unknown. I cherish my distant yet clear memories of that time.' He produced several townscapes in the first years of the 20th century, which he based partly on prints and partly on his own imagination. He tried hard to avoid the city itself and if he was obliged to go there, he claims to have worn dark glasses so that he would not have to see what had become of his city.

Khnopff's emotional ties with Bruges are expressed in a complex manner in *Secret-Reflet* (Secret-Reflection). The woman is Bruges. Her encounter with her stone image is paralleled in the lower picture by the reflection of St John's Hospital in the water. Khnopff's work is invariably charged with deeper psychological meaning, as we find here with the narcissistic relationship between the woman and her unfathomable and secret self. The artist identifies with the woman and hence with Bruges.

Khnopff's buildings are often deliberately truncated, exchanging roofs and sky for additional space in which to concentrate on the reflection of the façades in the canal.

The artist summed up the philosophy behind this key work of Belgian Symbolism in the following words: 'Our life is in the past, our desires in the future. There is no present. What we call existence is the interweaving of our memories and hopes. Only dreams are real and eternal.'

Fernand Khnopff's favourite model was his sister Marguerite. Dressed in flowing robes and striking mysterious poses, she appears in many of his works

Idealist Symbolists shared a mystical and profound sensibility, which frequently lent their work a religious flavour. *The Man-God* is a Symbolist interpretation of the Christian vision of the Last Day. Jean Delville handles the theme in an original way: Christ does not appear as Judge, ready to condemn, but draws all of suffering humanity towards him. The monumental painting was a preliminary study for a mural – never executed – at the Church of Notre-Dame de la Chapelle in Brussels.

Jean Delville was born in Louvain but spent a good deal of his life in Brussels. He began his career as a Realist painter, but quickly fell under the spell of Symbolism. He frequented esoteric circles, including La Rose+Croix – the society formed in Paris in 1891 by the charismatic philosopher Joséphin Péladan. Delville became the magus's most important disciple in Brussels. Several other Belgian Symbolists, including Emile Verhaeren and Fernand Khnopff, were attracted to Péladan's occultism and his religious and aesthetic theories. In 1892, Delville founded the artistic society 'Pour l'Art', which was made up largely of idealist artists. He built up an international reputation, was awarded the Prix de Rome and spent time in Italy. He also taught at Glasgow's School of Art and the Brussels Academy, supported a variety of artistic initiatives and was appointed director of the Mons Academy. His glittering career is evidence of the high esteem in which his allegorical and high-flown compositions were held.

Rik Wouters' last monumental
sculpture is an image of his wife
Nel. The figure is larger than life and
was cast in bronze in a series of
twelve. Rik Wouters began as a
sculptor before shifting his focus
towards drawing and painting. His
wife was his favourite model. As a
painter, Wouters was the leading
figure of Brabant Fauvism, producing colourful and sunny impres-
sions. His sculptures are either full
of movement or, like *Domestic
Cares*, robust and compact. They are
all extremely natural, while the
energetic style with which Wouters
modelled his figures gives them a
powerful inner charge. In spite of
his tragic death – from cancer of the
eye in the middle of the First World
War – his work is an exaltation of
life and love.

Construction in the Sphere 2 1917   Georges Vantongerloo 1886–1965
Cement, painted white, 33 x 25 x 25 cm

– the group founded in 1917 by Theo van Doesburg and Piet Mondrian to promote abstract design. The painters and sculptors associated with De Stijl pursued a pure, non-representational pictorial language capable of functioning as a kind of universal language in modern society and of reflecting the mystery and order of the universe. Vantongerloo produced several geometrical sculptures in 1917, in which he applied the principles of pure representation in three dimensions. *Construction in the Sphere* 2 is one of those works.

In 1927, Vantongerloo moved to Paris, where he continued to work into his old age. He created a highly original body of work, the central features of which were mathematical proportion and natural phenomena like light and cosmic forces.

The Groeninge Museum's Vantongerloo collection highlights all the facets of his career and is the most important publicly owned ensemble of his work.

The fundamental changes that began to occur in European art in the early 20th century were also felt in Belgium. Certain young artists grew tired of Symbolism's introspection and literary baggage and focused instead on colour and form. It was abstract art that produced both the most radical and least understood creations of that period. There was no coherent abstraction-ist school or movement in Belgium, merely a few individual experiments. This was the context in which Georges Vantongerloo's variant of constructivist abstraction emerged. It made the Antwerp artist one of the pioneers of modern European sculpture.

Vantongerloo spent the First World War in The Hague, where he was involved with De Stijl

Looking at this gentle, hazy impression of a fairground, it is not immediately obvious that Edgard Tytgat was one of the leading Flemish Expressionists. Before the First World War, he painted in an Impressionist style, with fluid brushstrokes and delicate colours. He was fond of popular themes like the fair. In the 1920s, by contrast, he developed a highly individual, naïve and spontaneous Expressionism. It is characterised by a linear and flat design in which he avoids the monumental vision and dramatic distortions witnessed in the work of other Flemish Expressionists. Imaginative, humorous, ironic, playfully

erotic, charming and tender are indeed more appropriate adjectives to describe Tytgat's paintings.

Tytgat was a born storyteller and his awareness of narrative is a crucial aspect of his work. The fact that he was a townsman and spent most of his life in the suburbs of Brussels also influenced his imagery. His landscapes are always peopled with human figures. Tytgat's paintings recount minor events and entertainments like the fairground and the circus, but he was also inspired by barbaric and erotic Oriental tales, which he blended with his own, strange fantasies.

Edgard Tytgat's Expressionism was closely linked to popular art. He combines sharp outlines with almost uniform areas of colour to tell his tales in an almost child-like manner

Constant Permeke created imposing images of farmers and the fertile
earth in a monumental style and a
palette dominated by bluish blacks
and browns. Unlike Tytgat, he did
not see the countryside merely as
the setting for pleasant Sunday
strolls, but as the place where farmers engaged in their heavy toil. He
evoked that rural existence in all its
primitive grandeur. The element of
simplification and caricature lends a

penetrating, expressive power to
works like *Man Eating Milk-Soup.*
    Permeke was born in Antwerp
but moved with his family to
Ostend as a boy. In the years before
the First World War, he spent time
in the village of Sint-Martens-
Latem on the river Lys, where he
formed the 'second group of Latem'
with artists like Albert Servaes,
Gustave De Smet and Frits Van den
Berghe. These figures later became

the leading lights of the Flemish
Expressionist movement. From
1930 onwards, Permeke lived and
worked in the village of Jabbeke,
between Ostend and Bruges. His
house there is now a museum
(Provinciaal Museum Constant
Permeke).

Although this canvas was probably influenced by the annual fair in Ghent, where Gustave De Smet lived, there is more going on here than simply a desire to evoke the atmosphere and folklore of the fairground. The composition is highly synthetic – compressed into a space only a few paces deep. The shapes are influenced by Cubism and are sharply delineated. The colours have been reduced to shades of brown, red and ochre. The sober and expressive conception lends the work a monumental yet highly decorative character. This is not a picturesque scene but a timeless, interiorised vision. Gustave De Smet's Expressionism gave rise to a serene and genial body of paintings that express everyday life – primarily its happy moments.

The Ghent artist Frits Van den Berghe was undoubtedly the most complex personality among the Flemish Expressionists. As a result, his work is the most varied, displaying important stylistic developments and a wide range of themes. His work includes rural and village scenes alongside images of urban nightlife, and gentle gouaches and watercolours alongside sensual oil paintings. His initial manner, somewhere between Impressionism and Symbolism, gave way for a few years to a Cubist and Expressionist style, before being replaced in turn by a dreamy Surrealism, prompted by the energy of the unconscious.

During the 1920s – the period before he embarked on his Surrealist adventure – Van den Berghe moved from an extreme and dark Expressionism towards a restrained and harmonious art, dominated by robust volumes, warm colours and a mood of serenity, although a sense of unease is never too far away in his work. *Village Sweethearts* dates from this key phase in the artist's career.

life or snapshots of real landscapes? Is it his handling of sunlight and shadow, or perhaps rather his eye for the typical, sometimes trivial detail? And yet, the composition remains strictly geometrical. The outlines of people, animals, trees, objects and houses are sharply delineated patches of colour placed within a structured, formal pattern. Everything is reduced to taut lines, studied forms and colours.

Brusselmans was a solitary figure on the margins of Flemish Expressionism. He painted everyday life in his village of Dilbeek, near Brussels, and the landscape of Flemish Brabant. His son kindly donated a variety of his paintings to the museum, including an early work in the Fauvist style (*Woman at the window*, 1917).

Jean Brusselmans' affinity for reality makes his art especially attractive. Despite the stylisation and simplification of his work, we clearly detect the real life and real nature that it contains. But how does he convey the feeling that his paintings are scenes plucked from

Flemish Expressionism was one of the dominant Belgian schools after the First World War. The new art was not received enthusiastically by the public, but within artistic circles it was celebrated as an authentically Flemish mode of expression. It was supported by a number of progressive Brussels galleries – particularly Le Centaure and Sélection, which also published a journal devoted to it. Flemish Expressionism was not a homogeneous movement – each artist represented reality from his own point of view. Common characteristics include the figurative style influenced by Cubism, the relatively muted colours and the generally moderate degree of distortion, though Permeke was something of an exception in this respect. The work of the Flemish Expressionists was also marked by its sense of humanity and its strong links with nature.

In 1921, Gustave van de Woestyne launched a fierce verbal attack on contemporary spiritual art: 'Down with sugary, tame and obedient religious art! We are fed up with it – the Catholic Church is stuffed to the rafters with the stuff. When I enter one of our churches and see the modern decorations, statues and paintings, I am not edified or moved. On the contrary, I feel like cursing.' Saccharine-sweet Virgin Marys and angels may well have been one of the reasons for the occasionally aggressive and caricatured approach Van de Woestyne adopted in his religious paintings of the 1920s – a surprising trait for this gentle Symbolist, who was such an admirer of the Flemish Primitives, Pieter Bruegel and early Renaissance art. Van de Woestyne did not see any contradiction. He once wrote of early Flemish masters: 'What I love in their work is the immense contrasts – contrasts that I also find in lovely modern painters like Picasso.' The following extracts from a letter he wrote in 1920, offering advice to a young painter, provide an even clearer idea of his views: 'The artist should not attempt to imitate nature. He should give the image neither the proportions nor the bearing that we ordinarily see, but, on the contrary, that which is expressed by thought and emotion, rather than physical reality. The Cubists go even further: they want to express their emotions through forms that have never been seen before – in other words, they want to *create* forms and objects that are *truly new*. I am convinced that by following this principle, it is possible to create new works that are every bit as beautiful as those of artists in every previous age.'

This was the vision that produced *The Last Supper*, a key work from Gustave van de Woestyne's Expressionist period. The painting is conceived as a monumental fresco – a form of art in which the painter was very interested. Christ and his disciples sit closely together around a square table in a cramped room with bare brick walls and a floor with a chequerboard pattern. The setting is more reminiscent of a miniature theatre than a room. The figures have stylised yet expressive faces, while their hands are unnaturally large. The sense of constriction, the agitated mood and the simplicity of the setting are remarkably reminiscent of Hugo van der Goes' *Death of the Virgin* (p. 23).

Having trained as an artist in his native Ghent, **Gustave van de Woestyne** moved in 1900 to Sint-Martens-Latem, the village on the river Lys where an artist's colony grew up to which poets, painters and sculptors came in search of a new and meaningful art. Van de Woestyne's admiration of the technique and spirituality of the Flemish Primitives helped him to develop his own, mystical and religious Symbolism. He became one of the leading figures of the 'first group of Latem'. His contact with modern art led him after the First World War to develop a complex and occasionally acid Expressionist style. At the same time he practised a neo-Realist technique, in which he assimilated contemporary developments. The results of the latter include a number of marvellous still lifes.

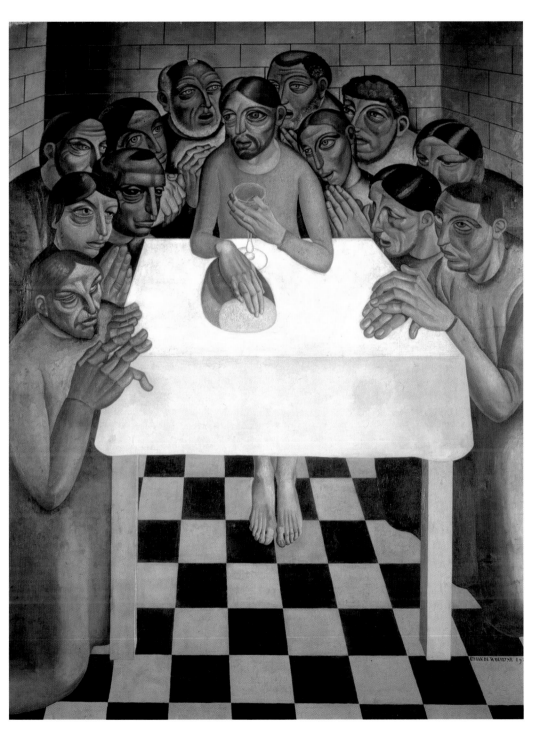

Although Paul Delvaux painted this canvas early in his career, when he worked in an Expressionist style influenced by Permeke and De Smet, we already recognise the dreamy atmosphere and beautiful, expressionless female figures of his later Surrealist work. By 1934 he had grown out of his Expressionist phase. His discovery of the art of Chirico and Magritte was a revelation that led him into the world of Surrealism.

The Surrealist movement was founded in France in the 1920s with the avowed aim of reconciling the 'previously opposed' states of dream and reality. It spread to Belgium around 1926 – a little later than Flemish Expressionism – and flourished particularly strongly in the French-speaking part of the country. The most original Belgian Surrealists were René Magritte and Paul Delvaux, who used a figurative style and precise painting technique to represent the world of dreams and the unconscious mind and to undermine the assumptions of everyday reality.

In his paintings, Delvaux creates a mysterious world full of classical buildings, stations and trains, with nude women in the foreground and set in unreal landscapes.

Serenity, 1970, panel, 122 x 152 cm, was specially commissioned for the Groeninge Museum by the Friends of the Municipal Museums. It is a late work that brings together the various characteristic elements of Delvaux's Surrealism, although it lacks the ghostly atmosphere of his earlier paintings

order to create a constantly shifting series of strange associations. Everyday objects take on a new life in these ambiguous images. Magritte forces us to revise, with him, our normal perception of real-

A female torso, a wooden floor, a painting within a painting, a neatly constructed block, clouds, a horse-bell and rows of curtained win-

dows. Beginning in the late 1920s, René Magritte gradually assembled his own pictorial vocabulary, from which he could draw as he saw fit in

ity – of existence itself. Our certainties are rocked on their foundations. He does so playfully, by making us his accomplices in word and picture games of which he has determined the rules. The title of the painting makes things even more confusing: we try to grasp the link between the image and the name given to it, but fail to do so as the title has nothing to do with the content. According to Magritte, reality and illusion are notions that can be mixed up – an idea he seeks to prove by means of unforgettable and poetic images.

René Magritte was born in the Belgian province of Hainaut. He entered the Brussels Academy at the age of eighteen. Magritte painted his first Surrealist works around 1925, having been gripped by his discovery of Giorgio De Chirico. Shortly afterwards, he settled in Paris for three years, where he took part in the activities of the Surrealist movement led by André Breton. Parisian Surrealism was not, however, the same as Magritte's brand and he returned to Brussels permanently in 1930. International recognition of his work grew strongly in the 1950s and beyond, and Magritte has been popular all over the world ever since.

The 20th century offered a greater variety of artistic styles and ideas than any prior period. New inventions, scientific discoveries and political revolutions followed one another in quick succession, prompting some radical changes in the world of art. Established values and standards were questioned. After the Second World War, the enormous development of production and which the Old World no longer sets the agenda. America became the laboratory in which experimentation took place and new movements arose. New York took over as the art world's centre of gravity. Yet despite this shift, many creative and original artists continued to work in Europe, some of them in Belgium, establishing international reputations in

communication techniques led to a hyperdynamic and internationalised society. Never before had society developed so rapidly as in the second half of the 20th century, never before had art been so turbulent. The most contradictory movements succeeded one another in brief waves. The postwar artistic landscape is a kaleidoscope of Figurative and Abstract Art, objects and readymades, Pop Art, Hyperrealism, Constructivism, Minimalism, Conceptual Art and much more. The principles of representation, aesthetics and the essence of art itself were explored and often emphatically rejected.

Belgium's art scene reflected international developments – indeed, the spirit of internationalism is a characteristic of the period. The whole of Europe, not to say the whole of the world, has become a melting pot, in

View of the room with the floor installation Untitled, 1993–94, and other works by Willy De Sauter (1938). De Sauter's interest in linear structures led to a constructivist phase, in which he worked with architectural forms. The sculpture Untitled confronts us with the alienation of modern housing systems.

the process. The Groeninge Museum has work by several leading Belgian figures and movements, ranging from Lyrical Abstraction and *Matiérisme* (Bram Bogart) through Geometric Abstraction (Dan Van Severen), Minimalism (Amédée Cortier, Raoul De Keyser, Willy De Sauter, René Heyvaert and Gilbert Swimberghe) and *Nieuwe Figuratie* (new figurative art; Roger Raveel) to Conceptual Art (Marcel Broodthaers).

Roger Raveel, *Your World in my Garden*, 1968, two panels
(oil paint, mirrors and bird cage), each 200 x 200 cm

The Brussels painter Henri-Victor Wolvens is something of an outsider in the museum's contemporary art collection. His lack of interest in the avant-garde explains the outlandish appearance of his work among the artistic developments just before and after the Second World War. He moved to Bruges in the 1930s, where he became one of the most important representatives of 'Luminism' since Ensor. The Belgian coast offered him a pure light in an infinite variety of shades. His style is very direct, with a dynamic technique and creamy handling of the paint. His favourite subjects are vibrant, sunlit seascapes and brightly coloured views of small towns, little stations, parks, terraces and interiors.

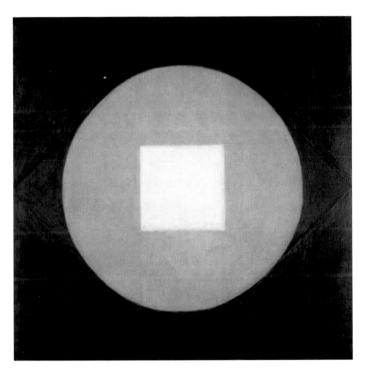

Dan Van Severen's art might well be described as ascetic. The essence of his work can be summed up as the pursuit of asceticism in order to achieve spiritual liberation. He restricts himself to elementary geometrical shapes like squares, diamonds, rectangles, crosses, circles and ellipses, which are arranged in such a way that they interact. Colours are limited to shades of grey in tempera or Indian ink. The simplicity of the composition helps create a kind of meditative art that relies on concentration rather than on laborious pictorial procedures. Van Severen sets out to achieve unity between pictorial matter and spirit; his experience is captured in a universal sign that encourages the viewer to reflect.

Genesis 1966–68

Roger Raveel 1921
33 works on paper, mixed media, each 55 x 73 cm
33 poems by Hugo Claus
Commissioned by the art collector Arthur Vandekerckhove,
who donated the series to the Groeninge Museum in 1989

Between 1966 and 1968, Roger Raveel produced 33 drawings devoted to the Creation story for the art collector Arthur Vandekerckhove. Meanwhile, Hugo Claus finished a cycle of 33 poems to accompany Raveel's drawings in October 1968. The resultant artistic and literary creation by two leading figures in postwar Flemish culture was published a year later as a limited-edition, loose-leaf book containing lithographs by Raveel and slightly amended texts by Claus. The book was designed by Philip Renard. The original drawings for *Genesis* were done in a variety of media and display Raveel's characteristically imaginative and colourful pictorial vocabulary: square and circle, tracks of colour, man and woman, self-portrait, hand, cat and pigeon, coffee-pot, car and bicycle, tree and wall, scribbles, dots, blocks, patches and lines. The chaos of signs gradually takes on meaning in the successive configurations. Little by little, the world is illuminated. Claus' poems are linked associatively with the images, but are by no means poetic transpositions.

Roger Raveel focuses on the difference between reality and illusion. Artists throughout history have occupied themselves with these two concepts, constantly finding new ways to address them. Raveel uses the pictorial idiom of his own time and allows figurative forms in his painting, yet he mixes contradictory styles and mocks traditional compositional schemes. He began to experiment in the early 1950s with combinations of abstract

signs and stylised forms that inter-
sect the real image. In later years, he
introduced actual objects into his
paintings – like the bird cage in *Your
World in my Garden* – and mirrors
that draw the viewer inside the
works.

The museum contains an exten-
sive Raveel collection that will provide you with an excellent insight
into the versatility of this painter,
draughtsman and printmaker.

New developments in art have the effect of disrupting the existing order. The resistance that people sometimes display towards contemporary art often reflects the difficulty they have in abandoning their traditional notions of art and the fact that they do not wish to be disturbed. They do not want to question things, at least not fundamentally.

Amédée Cortier began his career with dark, neo-Expressionist landscapes before evolving in the 1950s towards a stylised, figurative mode, dominated by lines and planes. In the 1960s, he began to produce an unusual form of minimal and geometric abstract art, in which colour took on its own emotional and spatial presence. Some of his paintings are entirely monochrome. Yet Cortier never lost sight of the fact that the space within a work of art is invariably linked to the space surrounding it – the place in which it is displayed. A painting can never be truly monochrome, therefore, as it hangs in a specific context; similarly, the three single-coloured parts of this triptych do not form an overall work that is monochrome.

The following analysis of the triptych was once offered: 'Cortier uses pure areas of colour to bring space to the viewer's attention, while simultaneously filling the human consciousness with intense colour.' Like Dan Van Severen, Amédée Cortier used simplification as a route to the essence. Both artists achieved a high degree of spirituality with a minimum of means, which is why this kind of fundamental, abstract painting was given the name 'Minimalism'.

Malmedy Series 1981–83

Raoul De Keyser 1930
51 (of a total of 121) brush drawings (with some pen, pencil, watercolour
and chalk), each 34.5 x 27.5 cm

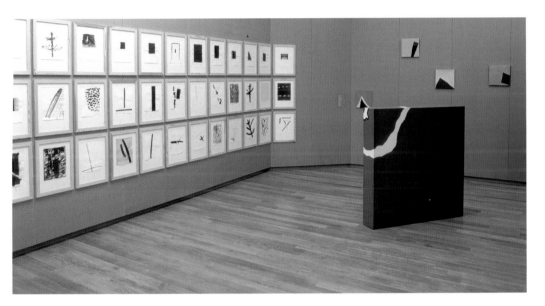

Raoul De Keyser began a series of works on paper in 1981. The first series of brush drawings dates from the years 1981, 1982 and 1983 and was given the title *Malmedy Series* after the Malmedy-Bond paper used by the artist. It comprises sheets of fine-grained typing paper, the surface of which is a little rough, giving the pencil marks something of a half-tone effect. The texture also provides a degree of resistance to a brush that is no longer sufficiently wet. Finally, the sheet has a tendency to crinkle as a wet drawing dries.

The *Malmedy Series* occupies a special place in De Keyser's work. There is little colour in the drawings, which are rendered primarily in shades of grey. The vocabulary of figurative, semi-figurative and abstract forms was drawn instinctively from his paintings, but also included new elements that crop up in later paintings. The series is not a composed ensemble but is made up of irregularly produced notes.

De Keyser was influenced at first by Roger Raveel, but subsequently evolved towards a more essential and compact mode of painting. Although this remained rooted in reality, its process of reduction led to a kind of figurative Minimalism. The identifiable motifs began to disappear in the mid-1970s, although the occasional echo remains. De Keyser became an abstract painter who does not express real experiences but encapsulates them as he paints. The more you immerse yourself in his work, the more you discover in it.

Through his objects, paintings, printed editions, prints, photographs and installations, Marcel Broodthaers questioned the meaning and nature of art, the artist, art theory, language, the museum and society itself. His chief weapons in his offensive against established values were literary ones – the written or printed word, associations between images and text, and absurd plays on words. He had, in fact, been a poet in his younger years, nurtured in the bosom of developments over the past few decades.

Broodthaers' career as an artist began around 1964, developing in parallel with international movements like Pop Art, Nouveau Réalisme (a French variant of Pop Art, which used everyday objects for aesthetic purposes) and Conceptual Art (for which the idea behind the work of art is more important than its appearance).

The different facets of Broodthaers' imaginative world are expressed in the printed editions that accumulated over his career to form an impressive series. They consist primarily of books, beginning with his first poetry collections in 1957 and followed by art books in 1964 and beyond. He began to make prints (typography, screen-prints and offset) that same year, and the collection also incorporates a number of objects on which he wrote or printed. The latter include a projection screen, bottles and the occasional piece of film. The Groeninge Museum's *Broodthaers Gallery* is the only publicly owned collection with a complete set of the artist's printed work.

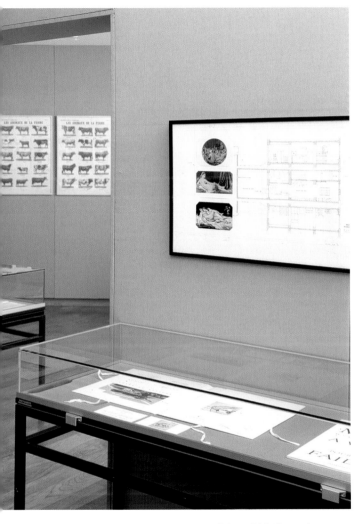

Surrealism, which focused a great deal of attention on the use of words in art. Broodthaers was also interested in printing and in everyday activities and *objets trouvés*. His shrewd, ironic and poetic work featured prominently in artistic

TEXT BOXES

The information in this guide is drawn from a wide variety of general and specialist publications. The following bibliography will be useful to anyone interested in learning more about a particular artist or movement:

Dirk De Vos, *Stedelijke Musea Bruges. Catalogus schilderijen 15de en 16de eeuw,* Bruges 1979.

Hans Vlieghe, *Catalogus Schilderijen 17e en 18de eeuw,* De Vrienden van de Stedelijke Musea Brugge, Bruges 1994.

Dirk De Vos, *The Groeninge Museum Bruges,* in the Musea Nostra series, Crédit Communal/Ludion, Ghent 1996.

Museumbulletin, Brugse Stedelijke Musea & Museumvrienden, bimonthly periodical.

Elisabeth Dhanens, *Van Eyck,* Mercatorfonds, Antwerp 1980.

Dirk De Vos, *Hans Memling,* Mercatorfonds, Antwerp 1994.

Elisabeth Dhanens, *Hugo van der Goes,* Fonds Mercator, Antwerp 1998.

Maximiliaan P.J. Martens *et al., Bruges and the Renaissance. From Memling to Pourbus,* exhibition catalogue, 2 vols, Stichting Kunstboek/Ludion, Bruges 1998.

Eva Tahon, *Lanceloot Blondeel in Bruges,* Stichting Kunstboek, Bruges 1998.

Van Bruegel tot Rubens. De Antwerpse schilderschool 1550–1650, exhibition catalogue, Snoeck-Ducaju & Zoon/Koninklijk Museum voor Schone Kunsten Antwerpen, Antwerp 1993.

Impressionism to Symbolism. The Belgian avant-garde 1880–1900, exhibition catalogue, London 1994.

Robert Hoozee *et al., Moderne kunst in België,* Mercatorfonds, Antwerp 1992.

K.J. Geirlandt *et al., Kunst in België na 45,* Mercatorfonds, Antwerp 1983.

Valentin Vermeersch, *Bruges, A Thousand Years of Art,* Mercatorfonds, Antwerp 1981.

Valentin Vermeersch (ed.), *Bruges and Europe,* Mercatorfonds, Antwerp 1992.

Herman Liebaers, Valentin Vermeersch, Leon Voet, Frans Baudouin, Robert Hoozee *et al., Vlaamse kunst van de oorsprong tot heden,* Mercatorfonds, Antwerp 1985.

Encyclopaedia Britannica 1999, CD.

I am grateful to the curators and staff of the museum, especially its director, Dr Valentin Vermeersch; Hilde Lobelle-Caluwe, curator; Laurence Van Kerkhoven and Eva Tahon, deputy curators; as well as to the Friends of the Municipal Museums of Bruges.

Copyright © 2000 Ludion Ghent-
Amsterdam and Irene Smets
Translation: Ted Alkins
Editing: Anagram, Ghent
Design: Antoon De Vylder,
Herentals
Typesetting: De Diamant Pers,
Herentals
Colour separations and printing:
Die Keure, Bruges
D/2000/6328/07
ISBN 90-5544-258-5

p. 124 Jan Provoost, *Donor's Wife with St Godeliva,*
detail (see p. 49)
p. 127 Emile Claus, *The River Lys at Astene,*
detail (see p. 90)

Gaspar-Peter Verbruggen the Younger, *Flower Still
Life,* detail (see p. 70)